Joy Meadow Cookbook
Recipes to Nourish the Body, Mind & Spirit

Joy Meadow Cookbook
Recipes to Nourish the Body, Mind & Spirit

Valencia Chan

ANGEL LIGHT PRESS
REDWOOD CITY, CALIFORNIA

Published by
Angel Light Press
709 El Camino Real
Redwood City, CA 94063

The information contained in this book is not intended as a substitute for consulting with your physician or health care provider. The publisher and author are not responsible for any adverse effects or consequences resulting from the use of any suggestion discussed in this book.

Designer (text and cover): Waldo Graphics, Redwood City, CA
Typeset in Adobe Usherwood
Photography: Valencia Chan, Kin Ho, Joseph A. Torres (in memoriam)
Printer (text and cover): Tin Shing Printing Co., San Francisco, CA

Library of Congress Control Number: 2004095438
Chan, Valencia
Joy Meadow Cookbook: Recipes to Nourish the Body, Mind and Spirit / Valencia Chan
ISBN 0-9759322-0-9

Printed in the United States of America.

Acknowledgements

I would like to express my heartfelt thanks to *Gail Waldo* for painstakingly typing my manuscript, written in long hand, and beautifully designing the book layout; deepest appreciation to my faithful staff who have been with me from the start of my restaurant in 1989 — *Ricky Wong* for his wonderful talent as head chef; *Kin Ho* for managing the dining room and keeping the building in working order; *Judy Jagerman* for her special touch in serving the customers; sincere gratitude to my parents, *Hoon Sing Chan* and *Yet Wah Chan*, for their encouragement and support; and finally, I am deeply indebted to my loyal customers who have made following my dream possible.

Much Blessings to all of you!

Valencia Chan

I literally grew up in the restaurant business. When I was two years old, my parents bought a coffee shop in the Haight and Fillmore area in San Francisco. In the pre-daycare era, my three older brothers, sister and I would just hang out in the restaurant watching and helping our parents. When I was eleven, my parents sold the coffee shop to start a Mandarin restaurant on Clement Street in the Richmond District of San Francisco. Being a great entrepreneur, my father started the restaurant with virtually no customers and eventually established a successful chain with ten locations in the Bay Area. He named the restaurant after my mother, *Yet Wah*, which translates to *Bright Moon*. In business since 1969, *Yet Wah* is still one of the most successful Chinese restaurants in San Francisco.

My parents have always been my greatest inspiration. They came to this country with no contacts, very little money and an inability to speak the language. With hard work and perseverence, they were able to raise five children and create a comfortable life for themselves. When my friends comment on how hard I work, I am truly humbled by what *real* diligence is.

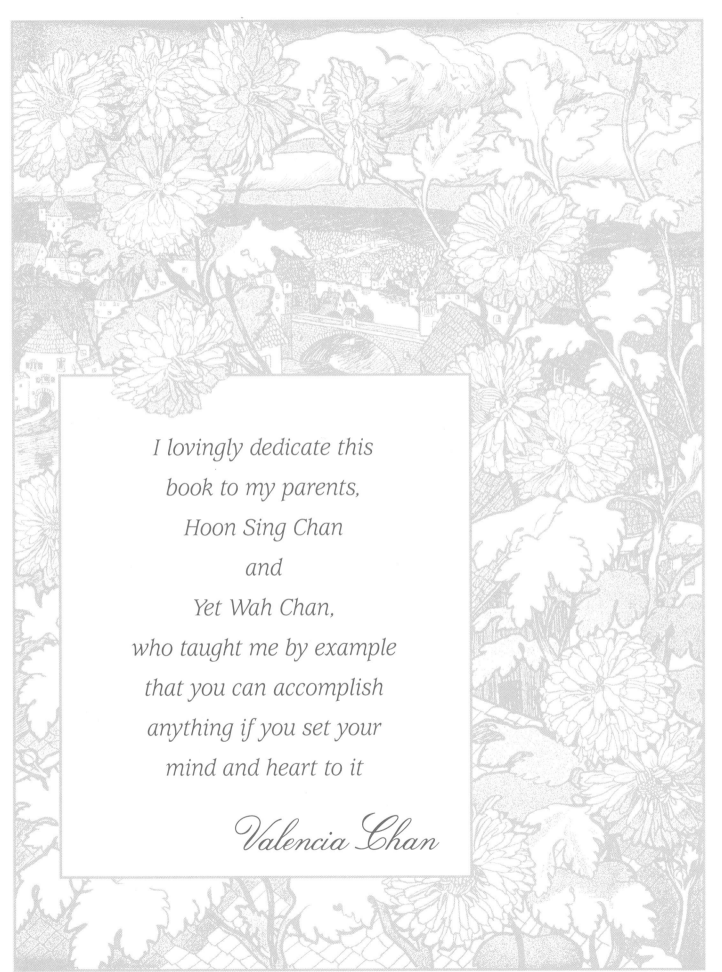

*I lovingly dedicate this
book to my parents,
Hoon Sing Chan
and
Yet Wah Chan,
who taught me by example
that you can accomplish
anything if you set your
mind and heart to it*

Valencia Chan

Visit us at

Joy Meadow Restaurant
701 El Camino Real
Redwood City, CA 94063
(650) 780-9978
www.joymeadow.com

Angel Light Books & Gifts
709 El Camino Real
Redwood City, CA 94063
(650) 780-9900
www.angellightbooks.com

Temple of Light
703 El Camino Real
Redwood City, CA 94063
(650) 780-9040
www.templeoflight.biz

Table of Contents

Introduction

We are meant to live a soulful life. I describe soulful as being *at one with our soul* — where we are living our purpose *and* enjoying health, harmony and happiness. Somewhere along our path most of us have disconnected from our soul and drifted far away from our true essence.

I wrote *Joy Meadow Cookbook – Recipes to Nourish the Body, Mind and Spirit* as a reminder to reconnect with our soul on a daily basis. The book is inspired by my Temple of Light in Redwood City, which has served as a non-denominational sanctuary since 1989. Recipes from our Joy Meadow Restaurant seek to nourish the body, inspirational stories from Angel Light Books & Gifts strive to uplift the mind, and metaphysical principles from the Temple of Light endeavor to expand spiritual awareness. I hope this book encourages you to create your own haven and inspires you to live a soulful life.

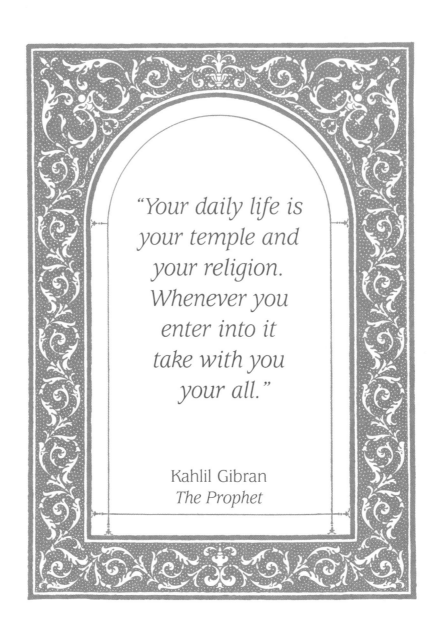

"Your daily life is your temple and your religion. Whenever you enter into it take with you your all."

Kahlil Gibran
The Prophet

Temple
of Light

Temple of Light

is a non-denominational center dedicated to promoting spiritual growth, healing and enlightenment. Established in 1989 by converting a dilapidated one-story building into a two-story sanctuary, it includes the Temple of Light, Joy Meadow Restaurant and Angel Light Books & Gifts.

Valencia Chan, proprietor and creator of the Temple of Light, believes that total well-being is a harmonious alignment of body, mind and spirit. At Joy Meadow your body is nourished by the healthful, delicious food; at Angel Light Books & Gifts your mind is stimulated by inspirational and uplifting books; and at the Temple of Light your spirit is renewed with meditation sessions and metaphysical classes.

The Temple of Light is located above Joy Meadow Restaurant. With its central atrium over-looking the Zen Garden below, it provides a tranquil setting for events and seminars. Also available are one-on-one healing and counseling sessions.

For our calendar of classes
and practitioners, please visit:
www.templeoflight.biz

"If opportunity doesn't knock, build a door."

—Milton Berle

For many years I was content waiting tables and managing my parent's restaurant. In the midst of it, I became a vegetarian and started to live a more spiritual life. The job no longer fulfilled me and I yearned to work in an environment that promoted total well-being by harmonizing body, mind and spirit. I envisioned a beautiful Temple with a Zen Garden as its focal point. Amongst its features would be a tranquil restaurant that offered a healthful style of cooking to nourish the body. An opening in the restaurant would connect to a metaphysical store filled from floor to loft with inspirational books to uplift the mind; a stairway would lead you upstairs to a peaceful sanctuary where esoteric classes were taught to renew the spirit. The ambience of the Temple would be soothing, healing and welcoming to people of all denominations. Wistfully I thought, "Too bad there isn't such a place for me to work in." Then it dawned on me: "Why am I waiting for somebody else to build it? I'm a somebody." The Higher Power that gave me the vision must also have the power to help me achieve it.

"You are never given a wish without
also being given the power to make it true."

—Richard Bach

"If you build it, they will come."

—Field of Dreams

In 1985, when I first saw the building that was to become my Temple, it was in a sorry state of disrepair. Never having been updated since it was originally built in the 1930s, it was worn and dilapidated. The bathrooms needed to be fixed, the roof leaked, there were bullet holes in the window, and graffiti on the walls. The block it was situated on was not good either. Among the businesses were three bars, an adult bookstore, a liquor store and a headshop (which was a new term for me). There was no parking lot for the businesses and the only pedestrians I noticed were panhandlers asking for money to go to the bars. The sole advantage to the property was that it was reasonably priced because of its distressed condition and seedy location. I had visions to completely gut the building and add a second story to include a spiritual teaching center, a counseling and a healing room, an apartment for myself in addition to the restaurant and metaphysical bookshop downstairs. I knew this could be an opportunity to fulfill my dream of building my Temple, but I was racked with doubts and fears. "Suppose I don't have the courage to live in the bad neighborhood by myself?; Perhaps this is the wrong location; What if no one came and I can't pay my mortgage?" Life would be easier if I just abandoned the whole idea and went back to my secure life. But ultimately my desires were stronger than my fears and I went ahead with my project. As it turned out, I did overcome my fear of living in the neighborhood by myself, some of the unsavory businesses eventually moved out, and on opening night and for a few years thereafter the restaurant, bookstore and Temple were packed with customers.

*"Real difficulties can be overcome, it is only
the imaginary ones that are unconquerable."*

—Theodore N. Vail

"Once you make a decision the universe conspires to make it happen."

—Ralph Waldo Emerson

When I designed the Temple, I had decided to build a one-bedroom apartment on the premises so I could save money on rent. Finally, after many months on the project, my contractor called to say that the apartment would be ready the first week of June. I knew it was time to sell my home so I could move into my new quarters. When I meditated on moving in Divine Timing, I received the message: *June 7*. I called a real estate agent that I got from the yellow pages and made an appointment to see her. When I told her that I needed to move by June 7th, she was flabbergasted and replied, "That only gives us less than one month to sell the house! Don't you know that it's a buyers' market now? I have homes that haven't moved in six months! Plus you need to put your home in a multiple listing, do open houses, wait for escrow to close…don't you know anything about real estate?" I replied, "I may not know much about real estate, but I do know when I get a strong message about something it always works out." I calmly said, "Give me your hands and let us affirm together: 'We now attract the perfect buyer in perfect timing, bringing perfect satisfaction for all concerned. Amen.'" The real estate agent shook her head and said, "Okay, we'll see what happens." She came back to put the "For Sale" sign up. When she got back to her office she had a message on her answering machine. A man had called to say that he just happened to drive by my street and saw the "For Sale" sign and was wondering if he could look at the house right away. After viewing my home he responded, "This house is exactly what I'm looking for. I only have one problem and I hope this won't kill the deal. Is there any way you can move by June 7th?" The real estate agent's jaw dropped. She looked at me and mouthed the words "How did you do that?" When you live a metaphysical life, you are more surprised when things like that *don't* happen.

"The person who says it cannot be done should not interrupt the person doing it."

—Chinese Proverb

*"All things whatsoever ye ask in prayer,
believing, ye shall receive."*

—Matthew 21:22

When I sold my home, the buyer had only one request, that I cleaned a stain on my cream-color carpet in my dining room. I thought, "Piece of cake…I'll just get some carpet stain remover at the store." No matter how I cleaned it, the spot would not come out. I thought about calling a professional carpet cleaner, but they required to clean a minimum of four rooms, which I did not need. I had enough to deal with packing that I turned it over to God. "God, I need to have this stain removed. I'll put this situation in Your loving hands and have You handle it. Thank You for answered prayers." The next day I was doing the dishes when the doorbell rang. When I answered it, there was a man standing with a carpet cleaner. He said, "Hi, I'm with Kirby Vacuum Systems. I am here to shampoo any room in your house absolutely free to demonstrate how powerful our new machine is." I laughed, "Thank You, God. I would have never thought of that!" I have never before or since had anyone offer that service to me.

There are no requests too trivial for God. When you have done all you can to no avail, let go and turn it over to God.

"The most important part of enlightenment is lighten up."

—Anonymous

"Vision is the art of seeing things invisible."

—Jonathan Swift

When I tell my clients to visualize their ideal life, they often tell me that they just aren't good at visualizing, yet they have no problem visualizing all the catastrophes that may befall them. But truly, what you hold in visualization does come to pass. Many prosperity books would suggest that you get a poster board and in the center put a picture of a spiritual symbol. It could be a picture of Jesus, an angel, the word *God*, or whatever you are drawn to place there. Around the poster board, paste pictures of what you would like to manifest. If it is a home you would like, put pictures of your ideal home, furnishings and garden. You could include affirmations on your poster, such as "I now manifest my ideal home" or "I am magnetic to my dream home." Every morning and evening, look at it…by the law of resonance, you will manifest it.

I have tried the poster board technique as well as visualizing what I want in my meditations. Both methods work wonderfully well. When I was putting my Temple together, it was such an ugly building that it looked hopeless to ever convert it into something beautiful. I didn't have the funds to remodel it, and it wasn't even zoned to add a second story. Because it was originally a one-story building, I could not double the size unless I could increase the parking. But every morning in my meditation I visualized a beautiful Temple with a Koi-filled pond and cascading waterfall, a two-story central atrium surrounded by lush foliage, and a bright and airy second floor devoted to metaphysical classes. Even when the architect gave me the disappointing news that a second floor couldn't be added, I had faith somehow my vision would come to pass. It was so clear and vivid in my meditation, I knew it was just a matter of time for it to manifest on the physical plane. Sure enough, miraculously, I received the bank loan, got the building permit, found an affordable contractor and, little by little, the ugly building gave way to a beautiful, radiant Temple. Just as I envisioned.

"A rock pile ceases to be a rock pile the moment a single man contemplates it, bearing within him the image of a cathedral."

—Antoine de Saint-Exupéry

*"One man gives freely, yet grows all the richer,
another withholds what he should give and only suffers want."*
—Proverbs 11:24 RSV

I had learned about the ancient secret of tithing from Unity Church and from reading Catherine Ponder's book, *The Dynamic Laws of Prosperity.* Tithing involves regularly donating 10% of your income to wherever or whomever you are getting your spiritual inspiration. It is believed that as you tithe, you prosper because you are putting God first, who is the Source of your Supply. I was considering this principle during a time that I was setting up my businesses and money was extremely tight. To finance my venture, I had maxed-out all my credit cards totaling $45,000 in debt (this is something I don't suggest anyone do). My minimum payment, which amounted to more than $1,300, was due in a week. My businesses were not to open until the next month so I had no income whatsoever. I was sitting in the pew at Unity listening to the sermon, when the collection plate was passed around. I knew that however I was living my life up to this point was not bringing me prosperity, so on faith I placed $100 on the collection plate. Doing so would leave me with only $30, but I figured desperate times called for desperate measures. As soon as I did that, I felt my whole body tingle and heard a soft whisper say, *"Everything is okay. Trust. You will be Divinely provided for as you follow your path."* When I got back to the shop to set up, a woman knocked on the door. She wanted to purchase a crystal sphere. I showed her what I had but she said that they were too small to meet her needs. Suddenly, I remembered that I had a huge 12″ sphere in my office that I had purchased when I was more prosperous. She told me it was exactly what she was looking for and happily offered me $1,800 for it. I was able to pay my minimum credit card bills, tithe and have money left over until I opened up my businesses. I was never as desperate again because I followed the ancient secret of tithing.

*"Thou shalt remember Jehovah thy God, for it is
He that giveth thee the power to get wealth."*

—Deuteronomy 8:18

*"I know the price of success: dedication, hard work and an
unremitting devotion to the things you want to see happen."*

—Frank Lloyd Wright

When a teacher has a low turnout for a class at my Temple, they will
often ask me if they did anything wrong. It's not that they did anything
wrong *per se*, it is just that the playing field has changed so much within
the last decade. For instance, when I first started the store there were very
few books or information about a subject called *Feng Shui*. The teacher who
taught the class had a great turnout. Now there are literally hundreds of
books on feng shui, classes taught everywhere and free information available on the internet. I find the same holds true on all topics. Unless you are
top-notch at what you do, and have the *chutzpah* to shamelessly promote
your work all over town, you will not have the results you desire. Using
metaphysical tools like affirmations and visualizing a successful turnout
wouldn't hurt either. Gone are the days when a person can read-up on a
subject and teach a class successfully. Mediocrity has no place now that the
standard has risen and information is available ubiquitously. If teaching is
your calling, hang in there! Continue to learn as much as you can about
your subject and be a master in your chosen field. Discover the secrets to
successful marketing and giving great presentations. Have confidence and
persistence and eventually the door to success will open for you. As Beverly
Sills reminds us, "There are no shortcuts to anyplace worth going."

"It takes twenty years to make an overnight success."

—Eddie Cantor

"With God, all things are possible."
—Mark 10:27

In 1995, I had closed down my Temple because of illness and stress and opened an Angel Shop in the Sacramento area of California. Knowing that someone occupied my property, I thought I'd set up shop somewhere else and not include a restaurant and teaching center to minimize stress. I was only opened a few months when I received word from the people who had leased my property that they needed to break their contract. Because I was healed from my thyroid condition by then, I knew it was time to re-open my Temple. The only problem was I had signed a five-year lease for my Angel Shop. When I mentioned this to one of the other tenants, who had a pet grooming business a few doors down from me, that I wanted to break my lease, she replied, "You will never get out of your lease. I have requested to get out of my lease before and the landlord said no. I've had my business since the mall first opened seven years ago. This mall has never been fully occupied. Out of fourteen units, there are always three to four vacancies. If you want to break your lease you'll need a miracle." Well, I knew God and my angels' specialty is working miracles. I prayed, "If I am meant to resume my Temple, please open all doors." I wrote a letter to my landlord stating my need to terminate my lease. Every morning in my meditation I would envision many new tenants calling my landlord to rent his storefronts, until he had an overflow of tenants and could release me from my contract. About two weeks after I started my meditation, the landlord stopped by my shop. He inquired, "Do you still want out of your lease? I don't know what's going on, but for some strange reason the phone has been ringing off the hook. I have so many people interested in renting my storefronts, I have a waiting list. Since there is such a demand I can get a higher rent. Can you leave in two weeks?" I replied, "Sure, I've been collecting empty boxes so I can pack right away." As I was packing, the woman from the pet grooming business came by and asked, "What are you doing?" "I'm moving." I replied. "Thank you for telling me about the lack of tenants situation. I was able to create a reality that benefited all of us."

"Faith sees the invisible, believes the incredible and receives the impossible."
—Anonymous

"It is possible to own too much. A man with one watch knows what time it is; a man with two watches is never quite sure."

—Lee Segall

When I am truly fulfilled in my life, I find I need less material trappings to make me happy. Prior to starting my Temple, I lived in a charming three bedroom house in San Francisco, had a closetful of clothes and shoes, and drove a VW Golf. (Okay, the VW is nothing to brag about, but at least I had a car.) For the past 13 years I have lived in quarters less than 300 square feet. I haven't owned a car in a decade, and I only possess two pairs of shoes at a time, one black and one tan to match my clothes. By simplifying my life I have more time and money to live a soulful life. Every day I feel gratified that I am able to live my life purpose with a minimum of stress. Don't get me wrong—I think it is glorious to have an abundance of money and possessions. God wants us to be prosperous. As Jesus said, "It is the Father's good pleasure to give you the Kingdom." But I wouldn't want to sacrifice my inner peace to attain material possessions. I know too many people who have maxed-out their credit cards because they are buying up things to fill up their inner void. Doing so would perk them up temporarily, but when that wears off they need to buy more things until it becomes a perpetual cycle. If they would live a more soulful life, find the joy in simple things, and follow their passion, they would find that they are happier with far less material things in their life.

"How do you expect God to give you more if you are not happy with what you have."

—Anonymous

"My religion is kindness."

— The Dalai Lama

Soulful Living

Every day create some time to do what you enjoy. Curl up in a plush chair and read a scintillating book; stroll in your garden and admire the profusion of flowers in bloom; take a luxurious lavender-scented bath. You'll be surprised how the little things can refresh and replenish your soul.

Take time each morning to meditate and connect with your soul before you start the day. You will find that by doing so, the rest of your day goes much more smoothly. There are many excellent meditation tapes that can guide you to a relaxed state. Books on different meditation methods are available, so find the style that suits you personally.

Spend some time exercising daily. Take the stairs instead of the elevator. When you go out to lunch, park farther away or find a place within walking distance to burn off extra calories. Join a gym or do exercises that are free like jogging, hiking and riding a bicycle. Exercise not only benefits the body, it releases endorphins and helps uplift the mind and spirit as well.

Connect with nature by planting a garden. If you are not fortunate enough to have a plot of land for your vegetation, a delightful herb garden can be created on your kitchen windowsill. Flowers and shrubs can be placed in unique planters for a lovely container garden on your porch, patio or balcony. Bright red geraniums will perk up a cheerless windowbox. Even putting a cluster of plants in your living room will provide a tranquil oasis. Working with plants links you with the nature spirits and keeps you in touch with a Higher Power.

Keep a Blessing Journal. Everyday write something in your journal that you are grateful for. Include small things that happen throughout the day: a kind word from a stranger, a smile from a child, hearing your favorite song on the radio. Know that what you focus on expands. When you are having a challenging day, read your blessing journal and soon the positive things in your life will increase and the negative thoughts will wither away from lack of attention.

Create a sacred spot in your home, even if it's a tiny niche in the corner of a room, and set up an altar. An altar will continuously bless your home. If you have a religious affiliation, you can display things on your altar that correspond to your beliefs or, if your spiritual beliefs tend to be more eclectic, put items that have special meaning to you. Light candles, burn incense, pray, meditate…envision your home and loved ones being filled with a radiant light of protection.

Find beauty everywhere. There is no admission fee required to delight in God's creations. Watch the sun rise calling forth a brand new day. Take a walk in a forest glen and behold the enchantment of nature. Go to the beach and relish in the vast ocean rolling up to shore. Feel the warm sand caressing your feet. On sultry nights, gaze at the luminous stars against the backdrop of the midnight sky. There is beauty all around us, we just need to take time to appreciate it.

Give yourself permission to express your creativity. You don't have to be able to do it well before you try. Venture into new territories. Learn to sew, play the piano, sing, dance… Reverend Oliver Wilson said it best,

"The woods would have little music if no birds sang their song except those who sang best."

Develop the talents you already have. Even if you have a natural knack for something, unless you develop it you can reach a plateau and you stagnate. What are you naturally good at? Take a class on it. Further your skills. Who knows? Maybe one day you may earn a second income from it, teach it to others, or just have fun doing it as a hobby.

Live your life purpose. Make a list of the things you enjoy doing. What are you passionate about? How would you spend your time if given the choice? Begin to integrate that into your daily life, your vocation, or volunteer work. Your life purpose is not necessarily your career. Your purpose for being here could be to raise your children, take care of animals, or be a source of light to others. We all chose to come to this planet for a reason. What is your purpose? Do it. *Live it.*

Practice seeing the Light of God in everyone you meet. Remind yourself that we are all God's children. Greet other people with a smile and kind word. Take time to truly listen to them and offer words of encouragement and support. Show compassion and understanding towards others. Reach out to people in need. Be a human angel, and when you see your brothers and sisters fall, help them up. One day we may find that borders are unnecessary for we are all interconnected as God's family.

*Then I saw another angel ascend from the
rising of the sun, and he called with a loud voice,
saying, "Do not harm the earth or the sea or the trees."*

— Revelation 7:2-3

Soulful Thinking

*"All that we are is the result of what we have thought.
The mind is everything. What we think, we become."*

—Buddha

Our reality is created by our thoughts. Everybody plays by the same metaphysical law. If you want to know what kind of thoughts someone has, just look at their outer reality. Someone who has money problems has lack thoughts such as: "I'm always broke," "Money is tight," "I can't pay my bills." To get out of that dilemma, you need to "fake it 'til you make it," so to speak. Change your thoughts to: "I am prosperous," "Money flows into my life," and "All my financial needs are met easily and effortlessly." Soon your outer reality will reflect your new thoughts. If you have been thinking lack thoughts for some time, it takes more energy to change that belief. Try writing out the positive affirmations multiple times in a notebook every morning. Recite the positive affirmations repeatedly. Watch your words when you speak. When you catch yourself saying words of lack, change it to a positive affirmation. Use guided meditations or subliminal tapes about prosperity. Close your eyes and visualize yourself receiving large sums of money, paying your bills effortlessly, spending it on things you enjoy.

There is never anyone to blame when you use this metaphysical law. No one can get inside your mind and force you to have negative thoughts. We always have the choice in what we believe. I see so many people wasting their energy blaming others for their lot in life instead of actively creating their ideal reality. For instance, if you had a boss who didn't validate your work, start saying, "My boss appreciates and values my work,"

When every cell in your body is infused with that thought, it radiates out in your energy field until you can *only* attract *that* reality. There are three things that can happen: your boss starts to appreciate and value your work; the boss who didn't validate your work is replaced by someone who does; or you find another job where the boss does appreciate and value your work. (Notice that you don't include the name of your boss because you cannot control others.) It is the law of resonance. We are magnetic to what is in our own energy field. Start thinking positive, wondrous thoughts and watch your outer world shift to match your new beliefs. *Dare to think and dream in unlimited ways.*

"Change your thoughts and you change your world."

—Norman Vincent Peale

Connecting With Your Angels

Angels are God's messengers. Everyone has at least two angels that are assigned to them to guide them in their lives. When you connect with your angels on a daily basis, life becomes easier and more joyful. At your home, set up an altar with fresh flowers and angel items, or place angel figurines and pictures throughout to remind yourself of the presence of angels. If you want help from your angels you need only call upon them. There is a spiritual law that says angels cannot intervene unless you invite them. Ask them for assistance and pay attention to the messages you receive. You may hear a faint whisper within your thoughts, or someone may appear and offer you the help you need. They also communicate to you by giving you signs — perhaps through lyrics to a song you happen to hear on the radio; or turning a page in a book that reveals to you your answer; maybe seeing a rainbow reminding you all is well. Be open to the angels responding in a multitude of ways, for once you ask for assistance, they will respond one way or another. To learn to communicate with your angels, a wonderful book that has helped me immensely is *Angel-Speake: How to Talk to Your Angels* by Barbara Mark and Trudy Griswold.

Besides your personal Guardian angels, there are also specialty angels. Call upon the Angel of Protection when you are concerned about your safety. When my customers tell me they are afraid to go to their cars after dark because of the seedy neighborhood, I suggest that they call upon the Angel of Protection to walk with them. You can surround your children with the Angel of Protection when they go out.

Teach them to connect with their angels regularly. Give your child an angel medallion to carry in their pocket or an angel pendant to wear as further reminder of their angel's presence. Let them know they are Divinely Protected. It is better to teach your children empowerment than to infuse them with fearful thoughts. Call upon the Angel of Love if you need help in the romance department, or the Angel of Prosperity for financial concerns. When you are ill, the Angel of Healing can be a source of comfort, and for depression, the Angel of Joy can uplift your spirits. Most people know about the Angel of Parking Spaces. Prior to arriving at your destination, call upon the Angel of Parking Spaces to open up a spot for you. Invariably, a car will pull out or there will be a spot just when you need it. Do not think you are unworthy to ask for help, or that your request is too trivial. Angels love it when you incorporate them into your life for their purpose is to serve humankind. Just remember to give thanks for their assistance and show others the same kindness and love as your angels have demonstrated to you.

Connecting With the Nature Devas

Sit in the center of your garden. Call forth the Nature Spirits. Notice if you feel your body tingle, or sense the caress of a gentle breeze brush against your face. A leaf may suddenly fall upon your feet, or you detect a slight movement of bushes and flowers when there is no wind. Squint your eyes slightly and see if you can perceive the form of flower fairies or pixies. Some people see them as flickering lights darting around the flowers and leaves. Speak to them telepathically. Tell them you welcome them to your garden. Thank them for all the work they do to keep your garden lush and beautiful. Ask them if you can do anything for them. Listen to the messages you receive. The first impression, image or word you get is usually that of the nature spirits.

If you want to connect with the Tree Deva and are not fortunate enough to have a tree in your garden, go to the park or woods. Choose a tree with which you resonate. Look at the trunk and branches and see if you can discern the face of a Tree Deva. Feel the heartbeat of the tree by putting your hands on the trunk. Quiet your mind. If this tree could talk to you what would it say? Listen to the soft whisper in your mind and record the response in a journal. Write down whatever comes to you without doubting or editing it. Trust the message you receive. Develop a relationship with your favorite tree by visiting it often to share your love and reverence.

Enchanting World of Flower Fairies

Just as angels guard over humankind, fairies, gnomes, elves, brownies and sprites guard over the nature kingdom.

- If you are pure at heart, love your garden and plant organically, nature spirits will gravitate to your garden.

- Fairies like to dwell in gardens that are natural and undisturbed. Leave a small portion of your garden uncultivated and wild, dedicated to the fairies to do as they please.

- Most people know that talking to plants helps them grow. You are actually communicating with the plant devas and developing a rapport with them.

- Plant fragrant flowers that the fairy kingdom loves, such as lavender, honeysuckle, roses and lilacs.

- Accessorize your garden with fairy windchimes, plaques, statuaries and fountains to remind yourself that the fairies are present.

- Children are more prone to see the fairy kingdom because they have not lost touch with the imaginary realm.

- Birds and butterflies in your garden are indications that fairies are present.

- You know that nature spirits are at work in your garden when you notice your crops are sweeter, plants are lusher, and flowers more fragrant and vibrant.

- In Celtic lore, the farmers would leave gifts of gratitude for the fairy kingdom. Favorite treats among the fairies are sweet cake, milk, honey and butter.

- You can show love and appreciation to the nature spirits by honoring Mother Earth and helping with environmental causes.

The Enchanted Garden

When I changed my store name to *Angel Light Books & Gifts* I wanted to convert the unsightly courtyard behind my building into a magical fairy garden. The space had broken cement flooring with ugly fuse boxes lined up against the back wall. I covered the floor with earth-toned terra cotta tiles and built planter boxes with matching trellises around the perimeter of the courtyard. Climbing roses and purple and pink bougainvilleas were planted up the trellises to conceal the back wall. A side door was built so one can still have access to the fuse boxes. Every morning I would invoke the presence of the flower fairies to bring magic and enchantment to the garden. In my meditative state I clairvoyantly saw flickering fairies darting from flower to flower, coaxing them to bloom and grow. I clearly perceived the image of a gnome sliding down the wrought iron banister in my garden. He was about two feet tall wearing a green vest, white shirt, suspenders, brown pants and a red cap. "Wee!" he cried, "We have another place to play!" Nature spirits love to be invited and included in the creation of a garden. I dedicated the garden to them by naming it *The Enchanted Garden*, and accessorizing the space with an angel fountain, fairy windchimes, angel birdfeeders, fairy plaques and statuaries, and hummingbird pinwheels sprinkled throughout the planter boxes. I hung miniature outdoor lights to echo the light of the flickering fairies. For such a small garden there is much to behold: bright red geraniums stay in bloom all year long, fragrant roses continue to blossom way past their season, and multi-colored dahlias grow to gigantic proportions. People who are sensitive to energy often tell me they can feel the presence of the nature spirits there. 'Til this day I can still sense the wee people at work and play, and hear their gentle whisper beckoning me, *"Come frolic with us in The Enchanted Garden!"*

"We are seeking to nourish your consciousness to move into Oneness. This does not mean that you ignore the wisdom of a proper diet, but that you include the most important ingredients which are awareness and love."

— David Spangler, August 12, 1971
transmission on kitchen and food

Joy Meadow

Joy Meadow

At **Joy Meadow** we believe the optimum dining experience should stimulate all five senses. Gaze at our Zen Garden with its lush foliage and Koi-filled pond. Listen to the soothing sounds of our whispering waterfall. Immerse yourself in the fragrant aroma of fresh herbs and spices. Taste such delectable treats as Bag of Fortune — a crispy pouch filled with coin-sized tofu, zucchini, carrots and water chestnuts in a scrumptious Mandarin sauce. Relax as ambient music gently fills the background, nestling you in comfort. Leave your stress at the door. We have created a tranquil oasis for a harmonious dining experience.

For a copy of our menu,
please visit our website at
www.joymeadow.com

*"Choose a job you love, and you will
never have to work a day in your life."*

—Confucius

Growing up in the restaurant business, I knew I had a natural knack
for it, but what consumed all my spare time was my voracious pursuit of
metaphysics. I was certified in astrology, practiced feng shui, meditated
daily and took various esoteric classes. I wanted a career that incorporated
my spiritual interests as well as my restaurant background. With innovation,
and the belief that one should follow their bliss, I have my dream job where
I do what I love every day. Being a bookstore owner *and* a book aficionado,
I can choose amongst tens of thousands of titles and read to my heart's
content. I am always meeting other metaphysical people to share interests,
conversations and friendship. Owning a restaurant gives me the luxury of
ordering the most intricate item on the menu and within 15 minutes it's
ready, all without me having to cook, clean or do the dishes. The peaceful
and harmonious ambiance in the Temple always soothes my heart and
uplifts my soul. Oftentimes customers would ask me how I can work seven
days a week, 10 hours a day. When you are living your passion, you really
don't consider it work. As Kahlil Gibran says, "Work is love made visible."

"Make your vacation your vocation."

—Mark Twain

"We should not let our fears hold us back from pursuing our hopes."
—John F. Kennedy

It seems that for everyone that have found fulfillment by living their dream, there are hundreds that have not because they let fear stop them. Fear is normal. You wouldn't be human if you did not have fear. And oftentimes I wonder if that anxious feeling in the pit of my stomach isn't fear, but excitement. It is the same butterflies I get when I go out on a date with someone I'm interested in. Perhaps we should rename it and say, "Wow, I am experiencing exhilaration. I feel truly alive. I need to go further with this wonderful energy!"

Frequently, the person who is the most enthusiastic about teaching a class in my Temple is the one who doesn't show up! They rave about how excited they are to teach the class and what a wonderful opportunity it is for them. As it gets closer to class date, they would invariably call in sick and I would never hear from them again. *Fear* got the better of them. I know what that feels like. People sometimes think that because I own a few businesses that I am immune to fear, but that is not so. There is nothing scarier than putting yourself on the line and feeling that everything you've worked for is riding on that moment. The pressure is tremendous. I remember on opening night in my restaurant I was a nervous wreck. If I could have called in sick I would have, but being the owner there is no one to call. Besides, I was hocked up to my ears with debt at that point— not showing up was never an option. I knew the only way to *work through the fear* was to *walk through the fear* until I came out the other side. Each time I faced my fears head-on I slowly developed more and more strength.

"You gain strength, courage and confidence by every experience in which you really stop to look fear in the face… You must do the thing you think you cannot do."

—Eleanor Roosevelt

"Life is like a ten-speed bike, most of us have gears we never use."

—Charles Schultz

When I was planning my restaurant I wanted to hire a professional chef to create my menu. Even though I grew up working at my father's restaurant, I was never professionally trained as a chef, so I discounted the possibility of developing my own recipes. When I couldn't find a chef to work with, I started to tinker with my own ideas. I created dishes that were aesthetic to the eyes and pleasing to the palate. Each of the items were given unique names to match the ambiance of the restaurant. I allowed my creativity to blossom. Developing the menu turned out to be one of the most rewarding experiences of my life. I find that customers don't really care if your ideas come from a cooking school as long as they enjoy it. We have since won many contests for favorite restaurant by receiving the most votes from readers of a local paper.

"Why not go out on a limb?
Isn't that where the fruit is?"

—Frank Scully

"The rainbow is more beautiful than the pot at the end of it."

—Hugh Prather

Oftentimes I hear stories about heirs to family fortune living a life of debauchery. Because money was just handed to them they never received the joy of following their passion. There is an emptiness in their souls that they numb by indulging in outside stimulation, which can never bring true fulfillment. In addition, by not earning anything in their lives, they never attained a sense of accomplishment. They would probably value a used car that they worked for, more than a Mercedes they were handed the keys to.

I am always grateful that my parents taught me responsibility and work ethics at an early age. From age eleven to age sixteen I worked in the restaurant kitchen after school, and from my teenage years to my early adulthood I waited tables. I was able to afford my first home when I was twenty-one because I saved all my tips for a down payment. By the time I owned my businesses, responsibility and perseverance just came naturally to me.

"The journey is the reward."

—Tao Saying

"Education is what you get from reading the small print on a contract. Experience is what you get from not reading it."

—Anonymous

Why is it that people who get a degree in business never open their own business? They know about theories and ideas of a business, but have no hands-on experience. The most successful business owners I know are usually self-taught. If you are naturally good at something, don't let not having a degree stop you. My father, who had no formal education or training in cooking school, was able to create an empire of owning ten Chinese restaurants at one time. When I was in college, I was so bored memorizing useless facts and statistics that served no purpose in my life, I couldn't wait until I got out. It wasn't until I left college that I expanded my horizon with the metaphysical knowledge that continues to serve me. For people who want to become doctors, teachers, lawyers, engineers…education does have its place, but there is a whole world out there where passion and experience are more important.

"The only thing stopping me from learning is my education."

—Einstein

"Every man is enthusiastic at times. One man has enthusiasm for thirty minutes, another has it for thirty days. But it is the man who has it for thirty years who makes a success in life."

—Edward B. Butler

I had an acquaintance who, upon losing her job, decided she wanted to open her own restaurant. Without much prior experience, she had no idea what she was getting herself into. Being an entrepreneur is hard enough, but I am told by bankers that the restaurant industry has a 95% failure rate. I advised her that, unless she had a burning passion to be a restauranteur, she should not do it. She was desperate to find a career and saw the restaurant business as something fun and glamorous, where she could invite her friends over to dine, meet new people, and have a place she called home. But she didn't have the passion nor enthusiasm for the business. Within a year she closed down her restaurant after losing all her investment. If you have the passion and zeal to do something I think you can overcome any difficult odds, but if your goal is just a passing fancy, you won't have the commitment and stamina to see it through.

"A man can succeed at almost anything for which he has unlimited enthusiasm."

—Charles M. Schwab

"We are living in a world today where lemonade is made from artificial flavors and furniture polish is made with real lemons."

—Alfred E. Newman

Sometimes I think the whole world has it backwards. The foods we consume the most are bad for us, the top-grossing movies often have no redeeming value, and tabloid magazines that focus on negativity are a multi-billion dollar industry. When my New Age friends tell me they don't fit in with society, I tell them, "Congratulations, maybe you are the one on the right track. Be true to yourself even if you don't fit in." Who's to say what is avant garde today won't be mainstream tomorrow? Someone has to be the pioneer.

I know in my own experience I would have more success if I gave the public what they wanted. For instance, the woman who works at the adult bookstore a few doors down from me boasts that they are so busy they have two salespersons on duty at all times, and the shop is kept open 24 hours a day to meet the demands of the customers. The bar and liquor store on my block always do brisk business. If I turned my restaurant into a bar and sold pornography in my shop I would be making a fortune. But that is not my calling and I have to be true to myself, even if I am serving only a small segment of the population.

"He who walks in another's tracks leaves no footprints."

—Joan L. Brannon

"Every problem contains the seeds of its own solution."
—Stanley Arnold

A woman came into my shop and inquired, "I heard you do feng shui. I have a problem. My house is infested with cockroaches—not just regular-size ones, but gigantic ones. Even after we have them exterminated they return. What do you think it is?" I replied, "Cockroaches gravitate where the vibrational energy is low." Of course, I didn't want to imply that she had bad vibes, so I tuned into the situation intuitively. I received the vision of a television set blaring with programs that were heavy and dense. I commented, "Your house is permeated with low vibration because of the negative programs you watch on TV. For instance, shows like *America's Most Wanted*, *Cops*…" Stunned, she replied, "Those are my favorite shows. I watch them all the time along with other similar programs. My father is hard-of-hearing so we have it on at full blast all day long." I advised, "If you want to get rid of the cockroaches, stop watching TV, clean up your place, light candles, burn incense, do prayer work, have meaningful conversations with your family. Perhaps the cockroaches have a message for you to live a more soulful life."

I should know about cockroaches. When I had leased out my restaurant during my illness, the tenants did not keep up the place. They had so many cockroaches and rats that the Health Department had cited them for numerous violations. They were finally shut down right during business hours, so all the food was left out in the kitchen. I was not looking forward to going inside. Since my tenants were paid until the end of the month and I did not have my keys back yet, I had a few weeks to work on it energetically. Every day I would meditate and surround the restaurant with light and love to uplift the vibrational frequency. As I did this, the space glowed with more and more light with each passing day. In my meditation I saw the image of the rats and cockroaches leaving in droves because they were not comfortable with the higher vibrational frequency. After a few weeks the tenants sent back my keys. I half-dreaded opening up the door to go inside. I knew that the rats and cockroaches had left in the astral realm, but I did not know if it had manifested in the physical plane yet. When I walked in, I noticed a stillness. They left. I looked all around and did not see them. Even though the kitchen had enough food for them to feast on for weeks, they had departed. Cockroaches have survived for eons, which goes to show negativity has survived for eons. To purify your space of negativity, clear out the clutter, keep it clean, surround it with light and love, and know you will only attract that of similar energy.

"Whatsoever a man soweth, that shall he also reap."

—Gal. 6:7

"Do what you know best, if you're a runner, run, if you're a bell, ring."

—Ignas Bernstein

I have no mechanical skills whatsoever. If the washer in the sink needs to be replaced, I have no idea how to do it. Changing the ribbon on our fax machine is a challenge for me. Meanwhile, my good friend and manager of my restaurant Kin, is a whiz at fixing anything. Whether it be the heater or refrigerator that needs to be repaired, he can pretty much look at it and figure out what to do. I, on the other hand, can dream up original menu ideas, feng shui the place and meditate like there's no tomorrow. Every morning before I open up the business, I would spend about one hour blessing the space with beauty, harmony, order and light. Kin sees the things I do as totally useless because it is less tangible than the things he does. He perceives me as helpless and incompetent and has no idea how I managed to stay alive this long. Kin is a left-brain, practical type, and I am a right-brain, intuitive type. We have different skill levels and need to respect each other's strengths instead of condemning each other's weaknesses.

How many of us are doing jobs we are ill-suited for and never use our innate talents to the fullest? How many of us expect our children to conform to a mold society has for them instead of honoring their natural-born gifts? I'm not saying that we shouldn't have them learn math or science if that is part of the curriculum, but we should not make them feel inferior if their talents lie elsewhere. If we can see everyone as being born with special gifts from God, we would value everyone's unique contribution to the planet.

*Each citizen should play his part in the community
according to his individual gifts.*

—Plato

Entrances to Joy Meadow Restaurant and Angel Light Books

The Temple of Light's unique round window

Angel Light Books & Gifts • The Angel Section

Angel Light Books & Gifts • The Candle Section

Angel Light Books & Gifts • The Statuary Section

Angel Light Books & Gifts • The Astrology and Tarot Section

41

Temple of Light entrance overlooking Zen Garden below

Temple of Light consultation room

The Temple of Light reception area

The Temple of Light conference room with view of atrium

The Enchanted Garden

The Enchanted Garden

The Zen Garden and Koi Pond

The interior entrance to Angel Light Books & Gifts

46

Soulful Eating

Eat fresh, whole foods whenever possible. Have the majority of your diet be alkaline-forming rather than acid-forming. Alkaline-forming foods are the fruits and vegetables, while acid-forming foods include meat, white flour, refined sugar, coffee and alcohol. People who consume an alkalizing diet with some added protein tend to look younger, feel more vibrant, and have fewer illnesses (the source of protein can be vegetarian). People who consume an acid-forming diet create a breeding ground for a host of ailments including heart disease, rheumatoid arthritis, migraine headaches and high blood pressure. The standard American diet tends to be overly acidic. It is no wonder that the health care and pharmaceutical businesses are multi-billion dollar industries. In Asia, where the population tends toward an alkalizing diet, people generally look younger, do not suffer from obesity, and rarely need to see a doctor. My grandmother from China, who lived to be in her nineties, never even visited a hospital, nor did she take medication of any kind.

There are thousands of diet books out in this youth-oriented, thin-obsessed nation, yet we are among the heaviest people, with more illnesses than less developed countries. The key is simple and natural — eat a predominantly alkalizing diet with some added protein, exercise, and live in moderation. You will look younger, feel more vibrant and glow with radiance and well-being.

While I believe for optimal health one should eat a predominantly alkalizing diet, I don't believe in extremes either. We once had a regular customer at the restaurant who was fanatic about following an alkalizing vegan diet. She would grill us about every single ingredient that was used in a dish. If an item had a trace of soy sauce or sugar, she believed she would become ill. She was so thin and emaciated one would think she was anorexic. Even though she was health-conscious, she looked weak and sick rather than vibrant and healthy. She had a miserable disposition, for the joy of eating was replaced by stress and strain. When she returned many months later, I almost did not recognize her. She was not as painfully thin, was more relaxed, and had a greater level of energy. Her doctor had warned her to ease up on her diet, so she started to incorporate other ingredients as well.

I think diet is one part of health, but just as important is the mind-spirit connection. If you think positive thoughts and center yourself with meditation regularly, your energy field is stronger. Even if you occasionally consume something less than ideal, it would have minimal adverse effects. People who are paranoid about every ingredient that goes in their body, and believe they will get sick if they eat the wrong thing, will probably manifest exactly that. Your thoughts create your reality. Stress, worry and anxiety contribute to more acidity and toxins in your body. For optimal well-being it is better to relax, take things lightly, and think higher thoughts. Do things that bring you joy and uplift your soul. Make healthy food choices, live in moderation and bless your meal prior to eating. Your body will respond with harmony, strength and vitality.

For many years I was a strict vegetarian, much to my mother's dismay. My body would periodically crave fish but, being a vegetarian, I did not consume it. Combined with stress and not listening to my body, I eventually developed *hyperthyroidism*. My heart was beating 120 beats per minute, I had nervous tension, insomnia and hair loss. My doctor said that hyper-thyroidism was very serious. Because of my rapid heartbeat he was afraid I would have a stroke at any time. He wanted to operate on me immediately and prescribe to me drugs that I would need to take for the rest of my life. Being a holistic health advocate, I was not about to do that. I went to a Chinese doctor who took my pulse and examined my eyes and tongue. He told me that I was depleted in zinc, and to incorporate fish in my diet right away. I followed his recommendation and took other supplements that I needed as well. Gradually my body restored itself. The swelling in my neck went away and my heart rate and other symptoms returned to normal. I know that there are many vegetarians who don't have any vitamin deficiencies. Everyone's body is different, and we go through various phases where we require certain nutrients. You need to follow your intuition and guidance on what is right for you. Listen to your body. Trust in the message it sends to restore you to optimum health and well-being.

"Love doesn't make the world go 'round.
Love is what makes the ride worthwhile."

— Franklin P. Jones

Soulful Dining

We live in such a fast-paced society our meals consist of prepackaged food, frozen food and fast food. We wolf down our breakfast while we make a mad dash to work; grab a burger at the drive-thru and eat while commuting; and ingest our dinner while watching the evening news. From time to time we need to replenish our body and soul by making our dining experience relaxing and pleasurable. To create soulful dining experiences, try some of these ideas:

On Sunday mornings, snuggle under the comforter and have a leisurely breakfast in bed. Include sumptuous treats like vanilla almond tea, fresh strawberries, oatmeal pancakes…

When the weather is balmy and the outdoors beckons you, pack a picnic and go to the park. Make it a delectable experience where all your senses are stimulated. Enjoy the fresh scent of morning dew. Listen to the birds sing. Behold the colorful tapestry of wildflowers in bloom. Sit by a majestic tree and feel its healing presence. Savor the crusty bread, luscious cheese, succulent grapes…

On wintry nights, sit by your fireplace on a blanket with your beloved. If you don't have a fireplace, light a profusion of candles and plop down on big cushiony pillows. Listen to rainforest music and imagine you are on an exotic island. Eat Moroccan food where no utensils are used, or have a smörgasbord of appetizers and finger foods…

Have a leisurely afternoon tea and invite your best friend. Take time to linger and share conversation. Pretend you are in a bucolic English countryside. Set the table with a colorful floral tablecloth and matching napkins. Fill a ceramic pitcher with a spring bouquet of daffodils and tulips. Use your pretty porcelain cups and plates to serve peppermint tea accompanied by cream of broccoli soup, watercress tea sandwiches and hot biscuits with lemon curd…

Occasionally create a five-star dining experience in your own home. Use your white linen tablecloth, fine china and polished silverware. Serve wine or sparkling cider in crystal stemware. Fold your cloth napkins into pleats to form a fan and secure with elegant napkin rings. Set your table with a bouquet of scented red roses. Dim the lights and play soft piano music. Be sure to conclude your dinner with gourmet tea and a scrumptious dessert…

Soulful Entertaining

One of our most lavish events is our Fall Fairy Festival. With the help of my friend Yvonne, we were able to transform the building into a magical, enchanting wonderland.

Butterfly balloons, pinwheels and banners heralded the event from outside the building. Inside, the shop was filled with an enchanting array of angel statuaries, fairy figurines, unicorn candleholders, dragon incense burners, and wizard snowglobes. Celtic harp music wafted through the shop creating a magical aura. Wishing wands and fairy dusts were given as keepsakes to our customers. A tabletop angel fountain was the grand prize in our free drawing. Next door at Joy Meadow, we adorned the Zen Garden with flickering fairy lights. Colorful balloons and fairy garlands festooned our banquet room, where an eight-course Fairy Festival Feast awaited our guests. A costume contest was held with the prize of a gift certificate to Joy Meadow Restaurant. Suggested costumes included angels, fairies, pixies, elves, gnomes, hobbitts and wizards. Upstairs at the Temple of Light, we hung fairy mobiles made from cut-outs of old fairy calendars sprinkled with glitter. Gracing our buffet table was a strawberry-vanilla sheet cake decorated with fairy picks. Two large fairy birdfeeders were filled to the brim with cookies and candies. Baskets of angel cards and fairy cards were displayed for guests to choose their message for the day. Metal folding tables were bedecked with colorful tablecloths, candles and crystals for our mystical fair. Angel guidance, clairvoyancy, mediumship, tarot and psychic readings were available for our guests. In another room, a massage table was set up for Reiki and hands-on healing. All the planning and preparations were well worth it, for people came from far and wide to partake in our Fall Fairy Festival.

Sharing food is a wonderful way to develop friendship and create a sense of community. At Joy Meadow, we have hosted many gatherings to share joy and sustenance with like-spirited people. Here are some soulful entertaining ideas inspired by our events that you can try at home:

Chinese New Year Tea Party

The traditional flowers for Chinese New Year are branches of plum blossoms in a tall vase. If you can't find plum blossoms, you can use a pot of fuchsia-colored azalea tied with a red sash for your centerpiece. Red and gold are the color scheme for the New Year—red for happiness and gold for wealth. Decorate your dining area with Chinese paper lanterns and fans. Next to each setting place a red envelope with a Chinese coin tucked inside for prosperity. On a pedestal plate display a pyramid of tangerines with the stems and leaves intact, a symbol of good luck in China.

Serve Chinese dumplings to indicate happy reunion, fish to signify prosperity, whole chicken to convey celebration, and noodles to represent long life. Fill a ceramic bowl with a mound of fortune cookies to bring positive messages for the New Year.

Rose Garden Tea Party

When roses are in bloom have a rose garden tea party. If you don't have space in your garden for outdoor seating, you can set your dining table with a bouquet of roses for the centerpiece and light rose-scented candles. A white tablecloth with embroidered roses would add a lovely accent. Carry the theme with plates and napkins that echo the rose motif. Play soft classical music. Sprinkle your food with organic rose petals. Cut tomatoes and radishes into shapes of roses and use as garnishes. Share idyllic conversation with other garden enthusiasts.

Radish Rose

 To make a radish rose, cut out four petals of skin around the radish. Drop the radish rose in a bowl of iced water to open out petals.

Tomato Rose

 To make a tomato rose, start at the base and with a sharp knife cut a thin spiral of skin all around the tomato. Beginning with the base end, roll up the tomato skin to form a coil. Sit the tomato rose on its base and spread the petals gently. Embellish with fresh basil to resemble the leaves of a rose.

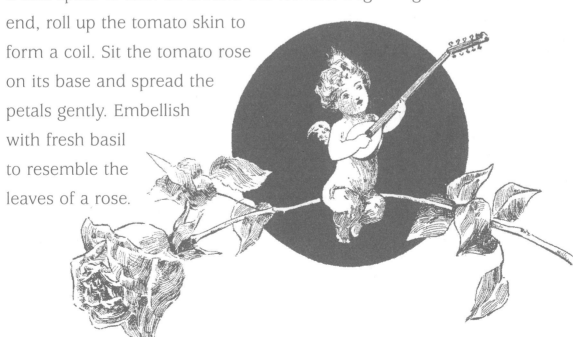

A Midsummer Night's Tea Party

At midsummer the sun is at its zenith and we enjoy the longest day of the year. It's a magical time of revelry when the fairies and wood nymphs come out to play as Shakespeare wrote in *A Midsummer Night's Dream*. Create your own merriment and allow creativity to flourish. Bring the alluring scent of jasmine, hyacinth and sweet pea indoors by snuggling them in small glass vases to perfume the air. Use your old-fashioned china tea set and have your guests dress in vintage clothing. Collect copies of *A Midsummer Night's Dream* from the library and invite your guests to participate in a play reading. Write the names of the characters on slips of paper and have your guests draw one. If the character is a minor one, your guest can take on two roles. Serve a buffet supper so your guests can nibble as the play progresses.

Harvest Moon Tea Party

The Harvest Moon is the first full moon that falls nearest the Autumn
Equinox. It is a day of celebration and giving thanks for all the abundance
in your life. Set the table bountifully with decorative gourds, dried ears of
corn, autumn leaves, and fall flowers such as zinnias and chrysanthemums.
Burn cinnamon and spice potpourri and light orange and russet candles.
Serve minestrone soup, stuffed squash, cornbread and hot apple pie. Have
each of your guests share what they are thankful for. It could be tangible
things as well as intangible things, such as inner peace, good health and
spiritual awareness. Gratitude is one of the laws of abundance—as you
give thanks it opens the door for you to receive even more.

Pray for Peace Tea Party

Hang flags, or pictures of flags, from around the world in your living area. Set the tone with a bouquet of Lily of the Valley, the flower for peace. Play James Twyman's *May Peace Prevail on Earth* or John Lennon's *Imagine*. Give peace buttons as tokens for your guests or make peace cranes with origami paper. Recite Saint Francis' *Prayer for Peace* together. Have someone lead a peace meditation. For dinner have a pot luck where each of your guests can bring a dish from their favorite ethnic restaurant.

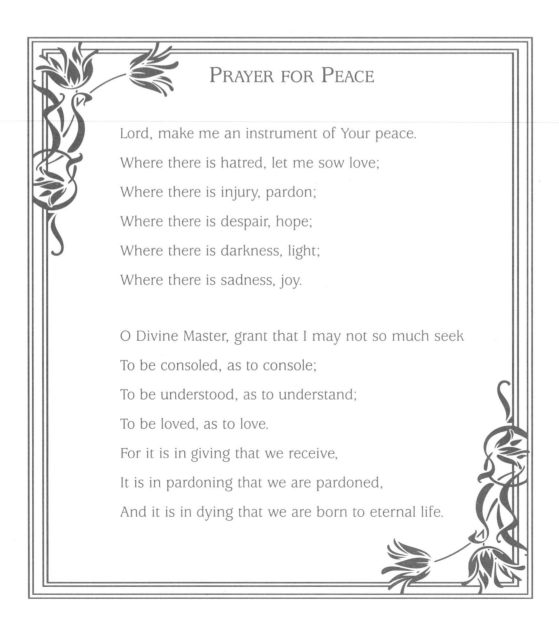

PRAYER FOR PEACE

Lord, make me an instrument of Your peace.

Where there is hatred, let me sow love;

Where there is injury, pardon;

Where there is despair, hope;

Where there is darkness, light;

Where there is sadness, joy.

O Divine Master, grant that I may not so much seek

To be consoled, as to console;

To be understood, as to understand;

To be loved, as to love.

For it is in giving that we receive,

It is in pardoning that we are pardoned,

And it is in dying that we are born to eternal life.

Guardian Angel Tea Party

Decorate your dining area with angel prints cut out from old calendars and mounted on poster boards. Bring out your collection of angel figurines and display them throughout your living area. For your centerpiece, set the table with heavenly perfumed flowers such as gardenia, roses, lilies or lilac. Light white candles on angel candleholders. Next to each setting place a small keepsake such as an angel ornament or angel pin. Play *Angel Symphony* by Merlin's Magic or *Gifts of the Angels* by Steven Halpern. Serve angel hair pasta with spring vegetables, garlic bread with rosemary, and angel food cake with fresh strawberries. Have each of your guests share stories of their encounters with angels, or an uplifting story of people acting as angels in their lives.

Fairy Wish Tea Party

Set your table with a mixed bouquet of fairy flowers, such as hyacinth, foxglove, bluebells and lavender. Hang miniature white Christmas lights throughout to reflect the flickering light of the fairy kingdom. Bring your fairy garden statuaries indoors to greet your guests. Play Celtic harp music or Irish folk songs to invite the spirit of the wee people. Make fairy wands and use them as place cards for your guests. Cut out gold stars and glue them onto cardboard. Secure on wooden skewers. Decorate the stars with sequins and stickers and write the name of your guests with color pens. As a memento, wrap glitter in pretty fabric and tie with matching ribbons to create fairy dust for each guest. Remind them to sprinkle fairy dust whenever they want some enchantment in their day. Be sure to include fairy cake and apple cider on your menu. Since fairies love butter, honey and milk, any cake recipes with those ingredients will do wonderfully. After dinner have each guest share their deepest wish. The group would then wave their wands and affirm that their wish will come true. This calls upon the exponential power of group prayer. As Jesus said, "Wherever two or more are gathered in My name, there I am." Expect miraculous things to happen as a result.

Joy Meadow
Recipes

*The more food your body
absorbs from the garden, the
better. As you eat, try always
to think of all those
who have helped with
the growing of the foodstuffs,
the devas, the nature spirits,
the angels; by doing this you
are showing your recognition
and appreciation for all that
has been done to help the
things grow here.*

— Eileen Caddy

Introduction to Joy Meadow Recipes

Chinese cooking has been renowned for centuries as being one of the finest cuisines in the world. They are famous for their 10-course banquets with each dish being unique and distinct. Every course contrasts between spicy and mild, sweet and sour, savory and subtle. Yet, when you look in a Chinese pantry, they use the same few ingredients—ginger, soy sauce, black bean sauce, hoisin sauce, rice wine and sesame oil. They were not privy to familiar herbs like thyme, rosemary, basil and oregano, nor dairy products like butter, cream and cheese. Until recent times they did not even have access to an oven. Everything from stir-frying, braising, steaming and deep-frying was done in a single wok.

As I am writing this cookbook, I am cognizant of how often I repeat the same ingredients, yet each dish is notably different. Since Joy Meadow is not a typical Chinese restaurant, I did take a few liberties in using some of the Western ingredients as well.

I hope you enjoy these recipes
and create for yourself
soulful dining experiences!

Glossary of Chinese Ingredients

Bean Threads – fine white noodles made from mung beans. Also called rice vermicelli and cellophane noodles, they are sold dried in small bundles and packets. Bean threads are often fried and tossed into Chinese Chicken Salad or presented as a bed of "snow" for sauteed dishes.

Black Bean Sauce – black beans fermented and preserved in salt and garlic.

Brown Bean Sauce – a thick brown sauce made from fermented soy beans, it is salty and pungent.

Chinese Chili Sauce – made from crushed fresh chili pepper and salt. There are many brands available, among the most common ones are Hunan chili sauce and chili garlic paste.

Five Spice Powder – blend of five ground spices made from star anise, Szechuan peppercorns, fennel, cloves and cinnamon.

Ginger Root – used extensively in Asian cooking, fresh ginger adds a spicy sharp flavor to dishes.

Glutinous Rice Flour – made from rice, it is used as a binding agent for recipes.

Hoisin Sauce – thick, reddish-brown sauce made from soy beans and flavored with vinegar and spices.

Oyster Sauce – thick, brown concentrated sauce made from ground oysters, soy sauce and brine. It doesn't taste like oysters but lends a rich, deep flavor to Chinese stir-fried dishes and gravies.

Plum Sauce – thick, sweet chutney-like sauce made from plums, apricots, garlic, vinegar and seasonings.

Rice Wine – made from glutinous rice, it is similar to sherry in bouquet and alcohol content, but with its own distinctive flavor.

Sesame Oil – amber colored oil pressed from toasted sesame seeds, it adds an automatic flavor to Chinese cooking.

Sesame Seeds – lend a nutty flavor to stir-fried dishes. Before using, toast sesame seeds in a pan over medium heat, shaking pan often until seeds are golden.

Shiitake Mushroom Sauce – Vegetarian version of oyster sauce, it lends a deep rich flavor to stir-fried dishes and gravies. Look for *Lee Kum Kee Vegetarian Stir-Fry Sauce* (mushroom flavored). For non-Vegetarians, if you can't find this flavorful sauce, substitute Oyster Sauce which is readily available in supermarkets.

Soy Protein – made from soy beans, it is an excellent source of protein, calcium and magnesium. It has zero cholesterol, almost no fat and is high in potassium and fiber. Though not a typical Chinese ingredient, it is often used as a meat substitute in Asian cooking because of its chewy consistency and meaty texture. Available in granules, slices and chunks, soy protein needs to be rehydrated in water before use. This versatile staple can be found in most major health food stores.

Soy Sauce – essential for adding a salty savory taste to Asian cooking, soy sauce is made from fermented soy beans, and water.

Tahini Sauce – paste made from ground toasted sesame seeds.

Water chestnuts – available in cans, sliced water chestnuts add a crispy, delicate flavor to dishes.

Cooking Procedure

At Joy Meadow, most of our recipes are cooked in a wok. We use a method called "pow wok," which means the flame is on intensely high heat. To keep the food from scorching, the chef lifts the wok up in quick successions. This seals in the juices and sears the food, making the flavor more pungent, and keeps the vegetables crisp. Since this is a very difficult method to duplicate at home, we have tested the recipes using a skillet on a stove to measure the cooking times. Please use the time indicated only as a guideline. Much will depend on the heat intensity of your individual stove, the type and size of skillet used, and the thickness of the ingredients being cooked.

Even though Joy Meadow is considered a health-conscious restaurant, you will notice that some of our recipes require deep-frying. When frying is done correctly, very little oil is actually retained. The food is crispy, yet not greasy. Since Chinese chefs did not have access to ovens until recent times, deep-frying is the authentic way to prepare many of their dishes. If you prefer, you can experiment baking some of the recipes that require frying.

JOY MEADOW

Vegetarian Cuisine • Chicken & Seafood Specialties

Menu

650.780.9978

www.joymeadow.com

701 El Camino Real • Redwood City, CA 94063

11:30am to 9:30pm — 7 Days

LIGHT AND TASTY

Spring Rolls

Crispy rolls filled with tender morsels of chicken, shrimp and vegetables . . . . page **86**

Imperial Rolls

Crispy rolls filled with julienned tofu, BBQ soy protein, snow peas, cabbage, zucchini, onions and carrots . . . . page **87**

Samosa

Crispy appetizers stuffed with potatoes, corn, peas and carrots in an Indian curry sauce. . . . . page **88**

Pot Stickers

Pan-fried vegetarian dumplings filled with tofu, vegetables and Asian spices . . . . page **89**

Yin Yang Delight

Vegetarian won tons prepared two ways, a bowl of our won ton soup and a plate of fried won tons with sweet and sour sauce. . . . . page **91**

Thousand Treasure Fried Rice

Rice stir-fried with a profusion of diced chicken, shrimp, mushrooms, corn, peas, carrots and broccoli. . . . . page **93**

Chicken Chow Mein

Chinese noodles stir-fried with julienned chicken, cabbage, onions, snow peas and bean sprouts . . . . page **94**

Tan Tan Noodles

Strips of tofu, mushrooms, cucumbers and carrots sautéed in a scrumptious tahini peanut sauce and topped over a hearty bowl of Chinese noodles . . . . page **95**

Oasis

Pita bread filled with tofu balls, alfalfa sprouts, tomatoes and lettuce, drizzled with an exotic lemon tahini sauce . . . . page **96**

Bodhi Tree

A delightful combination of eggplant, mushrooms and broccoli, sautéed in an aromatic peanut sauce and topped over a bowl of brown rice . . . . page **98**

Tang Dynasty

Vegetable tofu-balls, bell peppers, celery and pineapple bathed in sweet and sour sauce and topped over a generous bowl of brown rice . . . . page **99**

Wandering Monk

Tofu, potatoes, bell peppers and mushrooms sauteed in a flavorful curry sauce and topped over a hearty bowl of brown rice . page **100**

Satori

Slices of soy protein, mushrooms, zucchini and carrots sauteed in a nectarous tangy sauce accented with garlic, a touch of chili sauce and tangerine peel, served over brown rice . . . . page **101**

Sedona Sunset

Diced tofu, BBQ soy protein, mushrooms, carrots, green peas and broccoli florets exquisitely sauteed in a spicy chili sauce and served with brown rice. . . . . page **102**

Seven Petals

Seven different vegetables make up this delectable dish. Broccoli, cauliflower, zucchini, brussels sprouts, snow peas, mushrooms and carrots are sauteed with garlic, wine and herbs. Served with brown rice or lemon rice pilaf . . . . page **103**

Mushi Vegetable Crepes

Julienned tofu, shiitake and button mushrooms, snow peas, cabbage, zucchini and onions sautéed in a wok and wrapped in Mandarin pancakes with plum sauce . . . . page **104**

Mushi Chicken Crepes

Tender strips of chicken, cabbage, onions, snow peas, shiitake and button mushrooms, and eggs sauteed in a wok and wrapped in Mandarin pancakes with plum sauce. Served with a side of fresh fruit . . . . page **105**

Journey to India

A hearty serving of sliced chicken breast, bell peppers, onions and celery sauteed in a delectable curry sauce and topped over a bowl of white rice. . . . . page **106**

Shangri la Chicken

Slices of boneless chicken breast marinated in a delicious plum sauce and wrapped in foil. Served with Mandarin rolls . . page **107**

Nirvana

A heavenly bowl of Chinese noodle soup topped with a medley of chicken, shrimp, broccoli, Napa cabbage, snow peas, carrots, zucchini and mushrooms . . . . page **108**

Meadowlark

Shredded potatoes fried in the shape of a bird's nest and filled with boneless chicken breast, bell peppers, celery and pineapple in a tasty sweet and sour sauce. Served with brown rice or lemon rice pilaf . . . . page **109**

Seaport

Prawns, water chestnuts, carrots, zucchini and mushrooms sautéed in a robust sauce seasoned with garlic, chili and hoisin sauce, served over steamed white rice . . . . page **111**

SALADS

Tibetan Temple
Braised shiitake mushrooms, mixed salad greens, crispy noodles and cashews tossed in a delectable plum sauce dressing. Served with Mandarin rolls..................................*page* **114**

Cantonese Tofu Salad
Strips of braised tofu, mixed salad greens, cucumbers, carrots and crispy noodles tossed in an exquisite sesame-peanut dressing. Served with Mandarin rolls................................*page* **115**

Mediterranean Magic
Vegetable tofu balls, garden salad, tomatoes and spinach leaves topped with a scrumptious tahini dressing. Served with a multigrain roll..................................*page* **115**

Early Spring Chicken Salad
Strips of chicken breast, mixed salad greens, carrots, crispy noodles and cashews tossed in a succulent plum sauce dressing. Served with Mandarin rolls...........................*page* **116**

Cantonese Chicken Salad
Strips of chicken breast, mixed lettuce, cucumbers, carrots and crispy noodles tossed in an aromatic peanut and sesame dressing. Served with Mandarin rolls...............................*page* **117**

Sea of Paradise
A colorful tapestry of prawns, garden salad, seasonal fruit and glazed walnuts in an ambrosian honey mustard dressing. Served with a multigrain roll..........................*page* **118**

VEGETARIAN ENTRÉES

Autumn Harvest
An abundant harvest of broccoli, cauliflower, zucchini, baby corn, carrots, mushrooms, snow peas and cashews sautéed in a luscious black bean sauce. Served with choice of brown rice or lemon rice pilaf...................................*page* **119**

Bag of Fortune
Crispy pouch filled with coin-sized tofu, zucchini, mushrooms, carrots and water chestnuts in a Mandarin sauce flavored with ginger, hoisin sauce and chili sauce...........................*page* **120**

Buddha's Delight
Braised tofu, BBQ soy protein, broccoli flowerets, carrots, zucchini, mushrooms and green peas sautéed in a savory Chinese gravy. Served with choice of brown rice or lemon rice pilaf.....*page* **122**

Cupid's Delight
Heart-shaped napoletana made from layers of tofu, marinara sauce, zucchini, tomatoes, cheese and a delicate sprinkling of fresh basil. Served with seasonal vegetables and brown rice.............*page* **123**

The Enchanted Forest
Tofu sautéed in a succulent plum sauce and enticingly arranged with stir-fried broccoli. Served with brown rice or lemon rice pilaf...................................*page* **124**

Farmer's Bouquet
A bountiful pick of tofu, bell peppers, mushrooms, baby corn and zucchini marinated in an aromatic hoisin mustard sauce and broiled on skewers. Served with choice of brown rice or lemon rice pilaf...................................*page* **125**

Golden Chalice
A scrumptious creation of eggplant stuffed with vegetables and topped with a creamy béchamel or marinara sauce. Served with brown rice or lemon rice pilaf....................*page* **126**

Lotus Blossom
A harmonious blend of diced tofu, snow peas, celery, water chestnuts, mushrooms and ground nuts sautéed with a touch of Mandarin brown bean sauce. Served with lettuce leaves and plum sauce on the side to wrap, and brown rice...........*page* **127**

Midsummer Night's Dream
A culinary delicacy of croquettes made from walnuts, water chestnuts and carrots, sautéed in a sauce that is sweet, tangy and slightly hot. Served with brown rice or lemon rice pilaf......*page* **128**

Nepal Loaf
A nourishing vegetarian loaf made with tofu, brown rice, onions, carrots, celery and herbs, and topped with a flavorful mushroom gravy. Served with choice of brown rice or lemon rice pilaf.....*page* **130**

Panda's Village
Vegetarian version of the famous Mandarin Spareribs made from bamboo shoots and taro root topped with a tantalizing sauce that is sweet and savory. Served with snow peas, carrots and choice of brown rice or lemon rice pilaf.....................*page* **131**

Tofu Foo Yung
Patties made from tofu, snow peas, eggs, bean sprouts, carrots and celery topped with a delectable mushroom gravy. Served with choice of brown rice or lemon rice pilaf..............*page* **132**

Winter Into Spring
Soy protein sautéed in a fragrant plum sauce and beautifully presented on a bed of rice noodle "snow," with organic flower petal decoration.....................................*page* **133**

Zen Banquet
This innovative dish combines mashed potatoes with vegetarian stuffing shaped into pears – the symbol of longevity in China. Served with vegetables in plum sauce and choice of brown rice or lemon rice pilaf..................................*page* **134**

ENTRÉES

Ambrosia

Golden fried breast of chicken topped with a nectarous honey lemon sauce. Served with seasonal vegetables and choice of lemon rice pilaf or brown rice. . . . . *page* **136**

Bag of Fortune

Crispy pouch filled with a cornucopia of chicken breast, zucchini, mushrooms, carrots and water chestnuts in a spicy piquant sauce. Served with steamed broccoli and choice of lemon rice pilaf or brown rice. . . . . *page* **121**

Empress Chicken

A sumptuous dish of sliced chicken breast sautéed in a wealth of zucchini, broccoli, snow peas, mushrooms and cashews. Choice of lemon rice pilaf or brown rice. . . . . *page* **138**

Four Seasons Chicken

Slices of boneless chicken breast sautéed with ginger, garlic, hoisin sauce, basil leaves and a touch of chili sauce. Vegetables include broccoli, baby corn, zucchini and carrots. With choice of lemon rice pilaf or brown rice. . . . . *page* **139**

Five Happiness Chicken

Sliced chicken breast, bell peppers, onions, celery, zucchini and peanuts sautéed in a spicy garlicky chili sauce. Served with choice of lemon rice pilaf or brown rice. . . . . *page* **140**

General Tso's Chicken

Slices of boneless chicken breast, zucchini and carrots sautéed in a savory, sweet and tart Mandarin sauce. Served with choice of lemon rice pilaf or brown rice. . . . . *page* **141**

Jade Palace Chicken

Slices of boneless chicken breast sautéed in a fragrant plum sauce. Served with a garland of broccoli and cauliflower and choice of lemon rice pilaf or brown rice. . . . . *page* **142**

Starfire Chicken

Slices of boneless chicken breast, bell peppers, zucchini, celery and onions sautéed in a tangy spicy sauce. Served with choice of lemon rice pilaf or brown rice. . . . . *page* **143**

East Meets West

A medley of sliced chicken breast, prawns, snow peas, Chinese cabbage, shiitake mushrooms and broccoli sautéed in a wok and served over linguini. . . . . *page* **144**

Cape Cod Fantasy

Marinated calamari fried to a golden brown and served with seasonal vegetables and baked potato cake. . . . . *page* **145**

Seashore Surprise

Pan-fried calamari steak topped with a delicate sauce of lemon, wine and capers. Served with seasonal vegetables and baked potato cake. . . . . *page* **146**

Emerald Garden Prawns

Prawns sautéed with a colorful collection of broccoli, cauliflower, snow peas, zucchini, carrots and mushrooms in a mild garlic sauce. Served with choice of lemon rice pilaf or brown rice. . . . . *page* **147**

Neptune's Dream

Prawns sautéed in a heavenly garlic, wine and butter sauce. Served with seasonal vegetables and choice of lemon rice pilaf or brown rice. . . . . *page* **148**

Pisces Moon

Prawns exquisitely sautéed in a sauce that is sweet and tart with a hint of spiciness and arranged on a crispy white shell. Served with seasonal vegetables and choice of lemon rice pilaf or brown rice. . . . . *page* **149**

Midnight Seascapes

Prawns, scallops, garlic, bell peppers, onions and zucchini sautéed in a luscious black bean sauce. Served with choice of lemon rice pilaf or brown rice. . . . . *page* **150**

Jewel Sea

A colorful treasure of golden scallops bathed in sweet & sour sauce and lavishly garnished with seasonal fruit. Served with baked potato cake. . . . . *page* **151**

Appetizer Combo
Clockwise: pot stickers pg 89, imperial rolls
pg 87, samosa pg 88, tofu balls pg 97

Tan Tan Noodles
Page 95

Oasis
Page 96

Mushi Vegetable Crepes
Page 104

Meadowlark
Page 109

Tibetan Temple
Page 114

Mediterranean Magic
Page 115

Sea of Paradise
Page 118

Bag of Fortune
Page 120

Cupid's Delight
Page 123

Farmer's Bouquet
Page 125

Golden Chalice
Page 126

Lotus Blossom
Page 127

Midsummer Night's Dream
Page 128

Nepal Loaf
Page 130

Panda's Village
Page 131

Winter Into Spring
Page 133

Zen Banquet
Page 134

Ambrosia
Page 136

Four Seasons Chicken
Page 139

East Meets West
Page 144

Cape Cod Fantasy
Page 145

Neptune's Dream
Page 148

Pisces Moon
Page 149

"Dine by our soothing waterfall..."

Early Spring Chicken Salad and Sea of Paradise

I have included both a Chinese vegetable broth and an herbal vegetable broth because most households do not have some of the ingredients — like mung bean sprouts and lemongrass — readily available. When using vegetable stock in our recipes you can use either of these versions.

For convenience, there are many wonderful canned vegetarian and chicken broths available in the supermarket. If you are substituting with store-bought broth in the recipes, check the sodium content. If it is especially salty, dilute the broth with more water or omit the salt or soy sauce indicated in the recipe.

Chinese Vegetable Broth

9 cups water

2 cups mung bean sprouts

2 stalks celery, sliced

1 stalk lemongrass, chopped

1 carrot, sliced

½ onion, chopped

2 cloves garlic, halved

3 slices fresh ginger

1 teaspoon salt

⅛ teaspoon white pepper

Place all ingredients, except salt and white pepper, in a pot and bring to boil. Skim scum from surface then cover pot and simmer gently for 45 minutes. Strain stock through a fine sieve until just the broth remains. Season with salt and pepper. Cover and refrigerate for up to 3 days.

Herbal Vegetable Broth

8 cups water

3 cups coarsely shredded cabbage

2 stalks celery, sliced

1 onion, chopped

1 carrot, sliced

2 cloves garlic, halved

2 bay leaves

2 teaspoons Italian seasoning

1 teaspoon salt

   black pepper to taste

Place all ingredients, except salt and pepper, in a large pot and bring to boil then simmer gently, partially covered, over low heat for 45 minutes. Strain stock through a fine sieve until just the broth remains. Add salt and season to taste with pepper.

If you have your own herb garden, instead of dried herbs use fresh sprigs of basil, rosemary, marjoram, thyme, sage and oregano.

Marinated Tofu

32 oz. firm tofu (8 cakes, 4 oz. each) — drained

Remove excess water from the tofu by laying the cakes flat on a cutting board. Put another cutting board on top. Tilt boards slightly so excess water can drip out.

Marinade

Combine the following ingredients in a bowl:

$\frac{1}{2}$ cup vegetable stock

$\frac{1}{6}$ cup soy sauce

1$\frac{1}{2}$ teaspoons minced garlic

1$\frac{1}{2}$ teaspoons grated fresh ginger

Bake tofu in a preheated oven at 350°. After 20 minutes, turn tofu over to bake the other side for an additional 15 minutes. Remove from oven and pour marinade on top. Refrigerate for at least 4 hours, turning tofu over occasionally.

We bake the tofu first to give it a chewier consistency and meatier texture. When the tofu is firm it can retain the sauces better and withstand vigorous stir-frying.

Marinated tofu can be refrigerated for up to 4 days.

Marinated Breast of Chicken

8 oz. boneless chicken breast, cut into bite-size pieces
(except when recipes call for chicken breast to be halved,
shredded or diced)

Combine the following ingredients in a bowl:

1½ teaspoons water

1 teaspoon soy sauce

⅔ teaspoon vegetable oil

⅔ teaspoon sesame oil

½ teaspoon rice wine

½ teaspoon salt

½ teaspoon finely chopped fresh ginger

⅛ teaspoon white pepper

Evenly coat the chicken breast in the marinade and let sit for at least 15 minutes. Keep refrigerated if marinating for more than 15 minutes.

You can make a larger quantity of the marinated breast of chicken and keep in the refrigerator for up to 3 days, or in the freezer for a longer period of time. Prepared in advance, cooking will take just minutes.

Marinated Prawns

14 prawns (approximately 5¼ oz.)
   peeled, deveined, washed and drained

   Marinate with the following ingredients:
½ teaspoon vegetable oil
½ teaspoon cornstarch
¼ teaspoon salt
¼ teaspoon rice wine
⅛ teaspoon white pepper

Let sit for 15 minutes.

You can make a larger quantity of the marinated prawns and keep in the refrigerator for up to 3 days, or in the freezer for a longer period of time. Cooking will take just minutes if the prawns are prepared ahead of time.

BBQ Soy Protein

2 cups sliced soy protein
(soaked for 30 minutes to soften, then squeezed and
drained to remove excess liquid)

Combine the following ingredients in a bowl:

2 tablespoons hoisin sauce

1 tablespoon plum sauce

1 teaspoon minced garlic

1 teaspoon rice wine

1 teaspoon sesame oil

1 teaspoon ketchup

1 teaspoon finely chopped fresh cilantro

1/4 teaspoon black pepper

Add the soy protein and mix well. Spread the soy protein in a flat tray and bake in a preheated oven at 350° for 25 minutes. When the soy protein is baked with sauce it retains the flavor better and can be used in stir-fried dishes, like Chinese BBQ Pork.

BBQ soy protein can be kept in the refrigerator for up to 4 days, or in the freezer for a longer period of time.

Baked Potato Cake

4 medium potatoes (about 1 1/2 lb.)

1 clove garlic, cut in half

1 teaspoon butter

1 teaspoon salt

1/4 teaspoon black pepper

1 1/2 cups shredded cheddar and jack cheese, combined

1 1/2 cups milk

1 tablespoon butter

2 teaspoons finely chopped parsley

Cut potatoes into thin slices. Rub an 8 × 8 inch baking dish with the garlic clove. Brush baking dish with 1 teaspoon butter. Arrange potatoes in 3 layers, sprinkling each layer with 1/3 of the salt, pepper and cheese. Pour milk over potatoes. Dot with 1 tablespoon of butter. Bake uncovered in a preheated 350° oven until potatoes are tender and the top is golden brown, approximately 1 hour. Sprinkle with parsley.

Spring Rolls

6 spring roll wrappers
oil for frying

Follow the recipe for *Mushi Chicken Crepe* filling on
page 105, but substitute the egg in the recipe with ⅓ cup
shrimp that has been peeled, deveined, boiled and chopped.

Put about 2 rounded tablespoons of filling across the spring roll wrapper,
about 2 inches from the bottom edge. Fold the sides of the wrapper neatly
over filling, then roll up to enclose filling completely. Moisten around the
edges with warm water to seal.

In a wok or skillet, heat vegetable oil to 360°. Carefully add 3 to 4 spring
rolls at a time and fry for approximately 3 minutes, turning over as needed
until crispy and golden brown. Remove with a slotted spoon and drain on
paper towels. Cut spring rolls in half. Serve with a sweet and sour dipping
sauce if desired. Makes 6 spring rolls.

Sweet and Sour Sauce

Combine the following ingredients in a small bowl:

½ cup white wine vinegar
½ cup brown sugar, packed
½ cup ketchup
¼ cup orange juice
2 teaspoons cornstarch (diluted into the orange juice)
1 teaspoon soy sauce
1 teaspoon fresh ginger, finely chopped

Imperial Rolls

6 spring roll wrappers
oil for frying

Follow the recipe for the *Mushi Vegetable Crepe* filling on page 104.

Put about 2 rounded tablespoons of filling across the spring roll wrapper, about 2 inches from the bottom edge. Fold the sides of the wrapper neatly over filling, then roll up to enclose filling completely. Moisten around the edges with warm water to seal.

In a wok or skillet, heat vegetable oil to 360°. Carefully add 3 to 4 spring rolls at a time and fry for approximately 3 minutes, turning over as needed until crispy and golden brown. Remove with a slotted spoon and drain on paper towels. Cut imperial rolls in half. Serve with a sweet and sour dipping sauce if desired. Makes 6 imperial rolls. *Pictured on page 71.*

Brown Rice

1 cup brown rice	½ teaspoon soy sauce
2 cups water	¼ teaspoon salt
1 teaspoon olive oil	2 dashes white pepper

Rinse rice and drain. Put in a rice cooker with water. Cook until level goes to "keep warm."

In a hot skillet heat olive oil. Sauté rice with soy sauce and salt. Season with white pepper.

Samosa

Combine the following ingredients together:

  1 cup mashed potatoes (unseasoned)

  1/3 cup diced carrots, peas and corn (combined)

  1/2 teaspoon curry powder

  1/4 teaspoon salt

  1/4 teaspoon ground tumeric

  1/8 teaspoon ground cumin

  1/8 teaspoon ground coriander

  1/8 teaspoon ground marjoram

  12 pot sticker wrappers

     oil for frying

Put about 2 teaspoons of filling in a pot sticker wrapper. Moisten perimeter of wrapper with warm water. Fold wrapper in half over filling and crimp edges to seal. Fry in oil heated to 350° for 3 minutes or until golden brown. Serve with plum sauce for dipping if desired. *Pictured on page 71.*

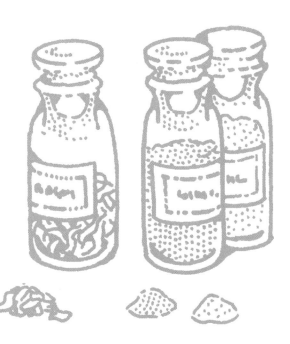

Vegetarian Pot Stickers

1 pkg pot sticker wrappers

4 *Marinated Tofu Cakes* (page 81), finely cubed (¼" cubes)

3 cups cabbage, finely chopped

1 celery stalk, finely chopped

⅓ cup onions, finely chopped

¼ cup carrots, finely chopped

2 teaspoons vegetable oil for sautéing

2 teaspoons vegetable oil for pan frying

2 teaspoons rice wine

1 teaspoon soy sauce

1 teaspoon fresh garlic, minced

1 teaspoon fresh ginger, finely chopped

1 teaspoon salt

1 teaspoon garlic powder

1 teaspoon sesame oil

½ teaspoon white pepper

Place a wide skillet or wok over high heat. When hot, add oil. When oil begins to heat add fresh garlic and ginger. Sauté for a few seconds to release flavor. Add tofu, onions, wine and soy sauce and sauté for 2 minutes. Add remaining vegetables, salt and garlic powder. Sauté 3 minutes or until vegetables are tender. Stir in sesame oil and white pepper. Put in a colander to drain out excess liquid. Allow to cool before wrapping.

Put about 2 teaspoons of filling in a pot sticker wrapper. Moisten perimeter of wrapper with warm water. Fold wrapper in half over filling and crimp edges to seal. Set pot stickers down, seam side up, so that pot stickers will sit flat. *Pictured on page 71.*

To cook pot stickers, put 2 teaspoons of oil in a non-stick skillet. Add pot stickers with ½ cup water and cook covered over medium-high heat until most of the liquid has evaporated. Turn down heat to low and continue to cook, shaking skillet frequently to prevent bottom of pot stickers from burning. When the bottom of pot stickers are golden brown and slightly crispy, remove from heat.

Serve pot stickers brown side up. For a dipping sauce, combine soy sauce, vinegar and hot chili sauce. Makes approximately 36 pot stickers.

Pot Stickers can be frozen, but be sure to space them apart so they won't stick together. When re-heating, cook while still frozen with a little extra water — if you defrost them first, they will be too wet and sticky to prepare.

Lemon Rice Pilaf

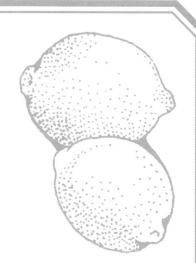

1 cup long grain rice
2 cups water
2 teaspoons margarine
1 tablespoon lemon juice
  grated rind of ½ lemon
¼ teaspoon salt
2 dashes of white pepper
2 teaspoons finely chopped fresh parsley

Rinse rice and drain. Put in a rice cooker with 2 cups of water. Cook until level goes to "keep warm." Heat margarine in a skillet and sauté rice for 1 minute. Add lemon juice and grated rind, stir until evenly distributed. Season with salt and pepper. Just before removing from heat, stir in chopped parsley.

Yin Yang Delight ☯ Vegetarian

1 pkg won ton wrappers

2 *Marinated Tofu Cakes* (page 81), finely chopped

½ cup onions, finely chopped

½ cup zucchini, finely chopped

½ cup celery, finely chopped

½ cup *BBQ Soy Protein* (page 84), finely chopped

⅓ cup carrots, finely chopped

2 teaspoons vegetable oil

2 teaspoons rice wine

1 teaspoon minced garlic

1 teaspoon ground ginger

1 teaspoon soy sauce

½ teaspoon salt

½ teaspoon sesame oil

⅛ teaspoon white pepper

In a wide skillet heat oil. When hot, add garlic and sauté for a few seconds. Add onions, tofu, soy sauce and wine and sauté for 2 minutes. Add remaining vegetables, ginger and salt and sauté for an additional 3 minutes or until vegetables have softened. Season with sesame oil and white pepper. Drain in a colander and allow to cool before wrapping.

Wrapping Won Tons for Soup

Put 1 teaspoon of filling in corner of won ton wrapper. Fold the corner over filling and roll to tuck point under. Dot the two side corners with warm water. Bring the corners together and pinch firmly to seal.

Wrapping Fried Won Tons

Put 1 teaspoon of filling in center of won ton wrapper. Moisten the edge of the wrapper with warm water. Fold diagonally to form a triangle and pinch firmly to seal.

> *Won tons for soup can be frozen. Be sure to space them apart so they won't stick together. To cook, boil them in their frozen state. If you were to defrost them first, they would be too wet and sticky to prepare.*

Cooking Won Ton Soup

Put the won tons in a pot of boiling water. Because the won ton's filling has already been cooked, it requires only about 2 minutes to boil. (Do not let the water boil so hard that the won tons come apart.) When ready, remove with a slotted spoon and place in a bowl. Heat 2 cups of vegetarian broth and pour over the top of won tons. Garnish with chopped green onions.

Frying Won Tons

In a wok or skillet heat 2 inches of vegetable oil to 350°. Fry 3 to 4 won tons at a time until golden brown, turning occasionally (2 to 3 minutes total). Remove with a slotted spoon and drain on paper towels. Serve with *Sweet and Sour Dipping Sauce* (recipe on page 86). Makes about 40 won tons.

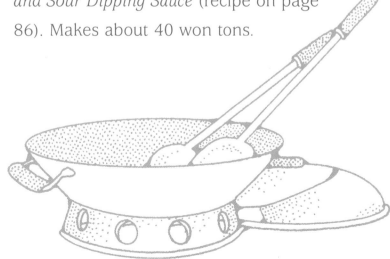

Thousand Treasure Fried Rice

4 oz. *Marinated Breast of Chicken* (page 82), finely diced

2 oz. *Marinated Prawns*, about 4 pieces (page 83), chopped

1 egg, beaten

1 tablespoon vegetable oil

2 cups cooked white rice

$1/3$ cup peas and diced carrots, combined

$1/4$ cup corn

$1/4$ cup button mushrooms, sliced

$1/2$ teaspoon salt

$1/2$ teaspoon soy sauce

1 tablespoon green onions, thinly sliced

2 dashes of white pepper

6 broccoli flowerets, steamed and set aside

In a wide skillet or wok heat 1 teaspoon oil over high heat. Sauté chicken and prawns for 1 minute. Remove and set aside. Heat 2 teaspoons of oil and scramble the egg. Add rice, salt and soy sauce. Stir in vegetables and continue to sauté for 4 minutes. Return chicken and prawns to skillet and stir-fry for 2 more minutes. Stir in green onions. Season with white pepper. Arrange on a large platter with steamed broccoli flowerets around the rice.

Chicken Chow Mein

9 oz. Chinese noodles, cooked *al dente*, rinsed and drained

5 oz. *Marinated Breast of Chicken* (page 82), cut into thin strips

2 teaspoons vegetable oil

1 teaspoon rice wine

1/2 teaspoon soy sauce

1/2 teaspoon salt

1/4 cup vegetable or chicken broth

3/4 cup cabbage, julienned

2/3 cup bean sprouts

1/4 cup celery, thinly sliced diagonally

1/4 cup onions, julienned

1/4 cup snow peas, julienned

1/6 cup carrots, grated

1/8 teaspoon white pepper

Place a wok or skillet over high heat, add oil. When the oil is hot, add chicken, soy sauce and wine and brown for 1 minute. Add vegetables and salt. Sauté for 1 or 2 minutes. Add noodles and broth and cook for 2 to 3 minutes. Stir in white pepper.

Tan Tan Noodles

8 oz. Chinese noodles, boiled until tender, rinsed and drained
2 *Marinated Tofu Cakes* (page 81), cut in 1/4″ strips
1/3 cup button mushrooms, sliced
2 teaspoons vegetable oil
2 teaspoons rice wine
1 teaspoon minced garlic
2/3 teaspoon soy sauce
3/4 cup vegetable broth
5 cucumber slices, cut in half to form half circles
1/8 cup carrots, grated
Tahini Peanut Sauce

Place a skillet or wok over high heat — when hot, add oil. When the oil is hot add garlic and sauté for a few seconds. Add tofu and mushrooms and sauté with wine and soy sauce. Brown tofu on both sides. Pour broth into the mixture and cook for 2 minutes. Add Tahini peanut sauce and stir until most of the liquid has evaporated, leaving a thick sauce. Put noodles in a large bowl and pour tofu mixture on top. Garnish with grated carrots in the center and the sliced cucumbers around perimeter. *Pictured on page 71.*

Tahini Peanut Sauce

1 tablespoon peanut butter, chunky-style
1 teaspoon tahini sauce
1/2 teaspoon rice wine
1/2 teaspoon soy sauce
1/2 teaspoon white wine vinegar
1/2 teaspoon sesame oil
1/4 teaspoon chili garlic sauce

Combine all ingredients until smooth.

Oasis

12 *Tofu Balls* (recipe on opposite page)
 1 cup alfalfa sprouts
 2 cups lettuce, chopped
 1 cup tomatoes, chopped
 2 pitas, cut in half to make 4 pocket breads, warmed in oven
    Tahini Lemon Sauce

Divide the tofu balls, lettuce, alfalfa sprouts and tomatoes into 4 portions and put inside pocket bread. Provide tahini lemon sauce to drizzle into the pocket sandwiches. *Pictured on page 71.*

Tahini Lemon Sauce

$1/4$ cup tahini paste
 3 tablespoons lemon juice
 1 tablespoon soy sauce
 2 teaspoons water
 2 teaspoons garlic, minced

Combine all ingredients in a small bowl.

Oasis Tofu Balls

In a large bowl, combine the following ingredients:

3 firm tofu cakes, well drained and mashed

$\frac{1}{3}$ cup carrots, finely chopped

$\frac{1}{3}$ cup water chestnuts, finely chopped

$\frac{1}{3}$ cup onions, finely chopped

$\frac{1}{3}$ cup celery, finely chopped

$\frac{2}{3}$ teaspoon salt

$\frac{1}{2}$ teaspoon dry oregano

$\frac{1}{2}$ teaspoon dry basil

$\frac{1}{4}$ teaspoon garlic powder

$\frac{1}{4}$ teaspoon white pepper

2 rounded teaspoons roasted peanuts, crushed

Add and mix well:

5 teaspoons cornstarch

5 teaspoons all-purpose flour

3 tablespoons dry bread crumbs

Roll into 1″ to 1$\frac{1}{4}$″ balls. Dust with additional cornstarch. In a wok or skillet, heat 1$\frac{1}{2}$″ of oil until it reaches 350°. Fry tofu balls for approximately 5 minutes or until golden brown. Makes about 20 tofu balls. *Pictured on page 71.*

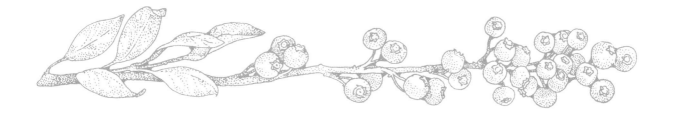

Bodhi Tree

2 Chinese eggplants* — medium-sized, about 5 oz. each

7 broccoli flowerets, steamed for 5 minutes and set aside

⅓ cup button mushrooms, sliced

2 teaspoons vegetable oil

2 teaspoons rice wine

1 teaspoon minced garlic

1 cup vegetable broth

½ teaspoon salt

½ teaspoon shiitake mushroom sauce (optional)

   Peanut Sauce (recipe on opposite page)

1½ cups cooked brown rice

Partially peel the eggplants, leaving some skin intact to give color and firmness. Cut into pieces 2″ long and ¾″ wide.

Add oil to a skillet or wok over medium-high heat. Sauté garlic for a few seconds. Add eggplant pieces and wine and sauté for 1 to 2 minutes. Pour in vegetable broth and cook covered for 3 minutes. Stir in mushrooms. Reduce heat to medium and cook covered for an additional 2 minutes. Add salt, mushroom sauce and peanut sauce, and stir until eggplants are tender and sauce well-blended. Pour eggplant mixture on top of brown rice. Garnish with steamed broccoli around the perimeter and 1 broccoli floweret in the center of the eggplant mixture.

* *Use the smaller Chinese eggplant for this recipe. If you use the larger American variety you will need to salt, rinse and drain the eggplant first in order to release the bitter taste.*

Tang Dynasty

6 *Tofu Balls* (recipe on page 97)

⅓ cup pineapple chunks

¾ cup *Sweet and Sour Sauce* (page 86)

1½ cups cooked brown rice

Boil the following vegetables in water for 1 minute, then drain
and set aside:

⅓ cup bell peppers, cut into 1″ squares

⅓ cup onions, cut into 1″ squares

⅓ cup celery, sliced diagonally ¼″ thick

Heat the sweet and sour sauce in a wide skillet over medium-high heat.
When it begins to boil, add vegetables. Stir in tofu balls and pineapple
chunks. Remove from heat and pour contents over brown rice.

*If tofu balls were prepared in advance, warm the tofu balls in oven prior to
stirring into sweet and sour sauce.*

Peanut Sauce

1 tablespoon peanut butter, chunky-style

½ teaspoon soy sauce

½ teaspoon rice wine

½ teaspoon white wine vinegar

½ teaspoon sesame oil

¼ teaspoon chili garlic sauce

Combine all ingredients in a small bowl until smooth.

Wandering Monk

2 *Marinated Tofu Cakes* (page 81), cut in 1″ squares, ½″ thick
2 teaspoons vegetable oil
1 teaspoon minced garlic
⅔ cup mushrooms, quartered
½ cup onions, cut into 1″ squares
½ cup bell peppers, cut into 1″ squares
½ cup potatoes — boiled, drained and cut into 1″ cubes
⅓ cup celery, sliced diagonally ¼″ thick
½ cup vegetable broth
½ cup Curry Sauce
¼ teaspoon sesame oil
   Cornstarch solution: 1 teaspoon cornstarch
   mixed with 2 teaspoons water
1½ cups cooked brown rice

Place a skillet or wok over high heat — when hot, add oil. When the oil is hot add garlic and onions. Sauté for 30 seconds. Add tofu and remaining vegetables and cook for 1 minute before adding broth. Cook for an additional 2 minutes and stir in ½ cup curry sauce. Add the cornstarch solution to seal in the flavors. Season with sesame oil. Serve Wandering Monk over a hearty bowl of brown rice.

Curry Sauce

Boil, then simmer, the following ingredients in a pot for 20 minutes:

2 cups water   ⅔ cup onions, thinly sliced
1 bay leaf   ⅓ cup lemongrass, thinly sliced

Strain stock through a sieve and add:

2 tablespoons coconut milk   ½ teaspoon salt
1 tablespoon curry powder   ⅓ teaspoon white pepper

Satori

1 cup *BBQ Soy Protein* (page 84)

1 teaspoon vegetable oil

1 teaspoon minced garlic

Savory Sweet Sauce

Cornstarch solution: 1 teaspoon cornstarch

mixed with 2 teaspoons water

¼ teaspoon orange peel, finely chopped

1½ cups cooked brown rice

Boil the following vegetables in water for 1 minute, then drain in a colander:

⅔ cup zucchini, sliced

⅔ cup button mushrooms, quartered

⅓ cup carrots, thinly sliced

Place a skillet or wok over high heat — when hot, add oil. When the oil is hot add garlic and sauté for a few seconds. Add vegetables. Stir in Savory Sweet Sauce. Add the soy protein, cook until sauce boils. To seal in the flavors, stir in the cornstarch solution. Sprinkle orange peel on top. Serve over brown rice.

Savory Sweet Sauce

Combine the following ingredients in a bowl:

½ cup water

3 tablespoons brown sugar

1½ tablespoons white wine vinegar

1 teaspoon Shiitake mushroom sauce

¼ teaspoon chili garlic sauce

Sedona Sunset

2 *Marinated Tofu Cakes* (page 81), cut into ½" cubes

1 cup broccoli, cut into 1" pieces

⅔ cup button mushrooms, quartered

⅓ cup diced carrots, corn and peas – combined

⅓ cup *BBQ Soy Protein* (page 84), cut into ½" pieces

2 teaspoons vegetable oil

1 teaspoon garlic, minced

2 teaspoons rice wine

1 teaspoon soy sauce

⅔ cup vegetable broth

¼ teaspoon salt

½ teaspoon chili sauce

½ teaspoon sesame oil

⅛ teaspoon white pepper

1½ cups cooked brown rice

Place a skillet or wok over high heat — when hot, add oil. When the oil is hot sauté garlic for a few seconds. Add tofu, broccoli, soy sauce and wine and sauté for 1 minute. Add broth, mushrooms, carrots, peas, corn and salt. Let cook for 2 minutes. Stir in soy protein. Add chili sauce and stir well.

When vegetables are tender, season with sesame oil and white pepper. Remove from heat and serve over a large bowl of brown rice.

Seven Petals

7 broccoli flowerets

7 cauliflower flowerets

7 snow pea pods

7 zucchini pieces, thinly sliced

7 carrot pieces, thinly sliced

4 button mushrooms, halved

4 Brussels sprouts, halved

1 cup vegetable broth

2 teaspoons vegetable oil

1 teaspoon rice wine

1 teaspoon Italian seasoning

1 teaspoon garlic, minced

   salt and pepper to taste

Heat a skillet or wok over high heat. When hot, add oil. When oil begins to heat add garlic and sauté for a few seconds to release flavor. Add broccoli, cauliflower, rice wine and broth. Sauté for 3 minutes. Add remaining vegetables and Italian seasoning. Sauté for an additional 3 minutes or until vegetables are tender. Season with salt and pepper.

Mushi Vegetable Crepes

4 moo shu wrappers (if unavailable, use flour tortillas)

1 *Marinated Tofu Cake* (page 81), cut into ¼″ strips

1 cup cabbage, julienned

½ cup zucchini, julienned

⅓ cup onions, julienned

⅓ cup snow peas, julienned

⅓ cup sliced button and shiitake mushrooms, combined

⅓ cup celery, thinly sliced diagonally

¼ cup grated carrots

⅓ cup BBQ Soy Protein (page 84), julienned

2 teaspoons vegetable oil

1 teaspoon garlic, minced

1 teaspoon soy sauce

1 teaspoon rice wine

⅔ teaspoon salt

⅛ teaspoon white pepper

4 teaspoons hoisin sauce

Heat moo shu wrappers in a steamer for 5 minutes. Allow to cool slightly before wrapping. Meanwhile, place a wide skillet or wok over high heat, adding oil when hot. When oil heats up, add garlic and sauté for a few seconds to release flavors. Add onions, tofu, soy sauce and wine and sauté for 2 minutes. Add the rest of the vegetables and salt. Sauté for 2 minutes. Stir in BBQ Soy Protein and cook for an additional 2 minutes or until vegetables are soft. Season with white pepper.

Spread 1 teaspoon of hoisin sauce onto each wrapper. Divide filling into 4 equal parts and place across the wrappers. Roll up and arrange on a serving platter. *Pictured on page 71.*

Mushi Chicken Crepes

4 moo shu wrappers (if unavailable, use flour tortillas)

5 oz. *Marinated Breast of Chicken* (page 82), finely shredded

1 cup cabbage, julienned

$\frac{1}{2}$ cup zucchini, julienned

$\frac{1}{3}$ cup onions, julienned

$\frac{1}{3}$ cup snow peas, julienned

$\frac{1}{3}$ cup sliced button and shiitake mushrooms, combined

$\frac{1}{3}$ cup celery, thinly sliced diagonally

$\frac{1}{4}$ cup grated carrots

1 egg, beaten

2 teaspoons vegetable oil

1 teaspoon garlic, minced

1 teaspoon soy sauce

1 teaspoon rice wine

$\frac{2}{3}$ teaspoon salt

$\frac{1}{8}$ teaspoon white pepper

4 teaspoons hoisin sauce

Heat moo shu wrappers in a steamer for 5 minutes. Allow to cool slightly before wrapping. Meanwhile, place a wide skillet or wok over high heat, adding oil when hot. When oil heats up, add garlic and sauté for a few seconds to release flavors. Add chicken, onions, soy sauce and wine and sauté for 2 minutes. Add remaining vegetables and salt. Sauté for 3 minutes. Form a well in the center of skillet and pour beaten egg into it. Cook until set. Stir the egg with the rest of ingredients. When vegetables have softened, season with white pepper.

Spread 1 teaspoon of hoisin sauce onto each wrapper. Divide filling into 4 equal parts and place across the wrappers. Roll up and arrange on a serving platter.

Journey to India

8 oz. *Marinated Breast of Chicken* (page 82),
cut into bite-size pieces

2 teaspoons vegetable oil

1 teaspoon garlic, minced

½ cup onions, cut into 1″ squares

½ cup bell peppers, cut into 1″ squares

½ cup potatoes — boiled, drained and cut into 1″ cubes

⅓ cup celery, sliced diagonally ¼″ thick

½ cup vegetable or chicken broth

½ cup *Curry Sauce* (page 100)
Cornstarch solution: 1 teaspoon cornstarch
mixed with 2 teaspoons water

1½ cups cooked white rice

In a skillet or wok, heat oil over high heat. When oil is hot, add garlic and onions and sauté for 30 seconds before adding chicken. Cook chicken for 2 minutes. Add vegetables and broth and sauté for 3 minutes. Stir in Curry sauce. Add the cornstarch solution to seal in the flavors. Season with sesame oil. Serve on top of a generous mound of white rice.

Shangri la Chicken

8 oz. *Marinated Breast of Chicken* (page 82),
     cut into bite-size pieces

Mix the chicken pieces in the following ingredients:

    2 teaspoons hoisin sauce

    1 teaspoon plum sauce

    ½ teaspoon ketchup

    1 teaspoon garlic, minced

    1 teaspoon fresh cilantro, finely chopped

---

    6 Mandarin rolls (Chinese bread)

    6 pieces of 6″ × 6″ aluminum foil

       oil for frying

Divide the chicken mixture into 6 equal parts and place them on the center of the aluminum foil. Fold the foil into a triangle and tuck the edges over 3 times to seal chicken inside the packet. Heat oil to 350° and fry the foil wrapped chicken for 4 to 5 minutes, or until chicken is cooked through. Serve the foil wrapped chicken with Mandarin rolls. To eat, remove the chicken from the packets and put inside the Mandarin rolls to create a sandwich.

Nirvana

5 oz. *Marinated Breast of Chicken* (page 82),
      cut into bite-size pieces

2 oz. *Marinated Prawns* (page 83), about 4 pieces

   ¾ cup Napa cabbage, cut into 2″ squares

   8 snow pea pods

   8 carrot pieces, thinly sliced

   8 zucchini pieces, thinly sliced

   4 button mushrooms, halved

   4 broccoli flowerets

   4 cauliflower flowerets

8 oz. Chinese noodles, cooked *al dente*, rinsed and drained
      and put in a large bowl or tureen

   3 cups vegetable broth

   ¼ teaspoon white pepper

   ¼ teaspoon sesame oil

Boil broth in a large pot. Add chicken, prawns and all vegetables, except snow peas. Cook for 4 minutes before adding snow peas. Cook for an additional 2 minutes. Season with white pepper and sesame oil. Pour mixture over top of noodles.

Meadowlark

Potato Birdsnest

2 cups potatoes, shredded lengthwise

2 tablespoons cornstarch

   oil for frying

Rinse potatoes and squeeze out excess water. Pat dry with paper towels. Place in a bowl and sprinkle with cornstarch until potatoes are evenly coated. Line a 5″ wire sieve (choose one with a long handle) with a handful of the potato mixture. Lay another 5″ wire sieve on top so the potatoes are trapped between the two sieves. In a wok or fryer, heat oil until it reaches 325°. Hold onto the handles as you gently lower the potatoes and sieves into the hot oil. Deep fry potatoes until golden brown, approximately 3 minutes. Remove from oil and allow the excess oil to drip out. Carefully remove the birdsnest from sieves. If the birdsnest does not come out easily, try tapping the side of the sieve to loosen. (If it still doesn't come out it could be an indication that the potatoes have not cooked long enough.) Set your birdsnest on the center of a plate. Makes 2 to 3 birdsnests.

Meadowlark continued
Sweet & Sour Chicken

Follow the recipe for *Ambrosia Chicken* on page 136, but cut the chicken into bite-size pieces before marinating and frying. Substitute the Lemon Sauce for Sweet and Sour Sauce (recipe on page 86).

Boil the following vegetables in water for 1 minute, drain and set aside:

¹/₂ cup bell peppers, cut into 1″ squares

¹/₂ cup onions, cut into 1″ squares

¹/₂ cup celery, sliced diagonally ¹/₄″ thick

1²/₃ cups *Sweet and Sour Sauce* (recipe on page 86)

¹/₂ cup pineapple chunks

Potato Birdsnests (page 109)

Heat the Sweet and Sour Sauce in a wide skillet over medium-high heat. When it begins to boil, add vegetables. Stir in fried chicken pieces and pineapple chunks until coated with sauce. Pour over the top of potato birdsnests. *Pictured on page 72.*

Seaport

4 oz. *Marinated Prawns* (page 83), about 10 pieces

³/₄ cup zucchini, thinly sliced

³/₄ cup mushrooms, quartered

¹/₃ cup carrots, thinly sliced

¹/₃ cup water chestnuts

2 teaspoons vegetable oil

3 ginger slices

1 teaspoon garlic, minced

1 teaspoon rice wine

²/₃ cup vegetable or chicken broth

1 teaspoon hoisin sauce

¹/₄ teaspoon chili sauce

1 teaspoon fresh basil, finely chopped

Cornstarch solution: 1 teaspoon cornstarch

mixed with 2 teaspoons water

1¹/₂ cups cooked white rice

Heat a skillet with oil. When hot, add ginger and garlic. Sauté for a few seconds before adding prawns. Cook over medium-high heat for 1 minute, flipping prawns over as they turn pink. Add wine. Stir in vegetables and sauté for 1 minute. Add broth and cook an additional 2 to 3 minutes. Stir in hoisin sauce and chili sauce. Add the cornstarch solution to seal in the flavor of the sauces. Sprinkle with fresh basil. Serve with white rice.

Ingredients for Salads

Mixed Salad Greens

Wash, dry and toss the following ingredients:

1/2 Romaine lettuce head, cut into 1″ to 2″ pieces

1/4 iceberg lettuce head, cut into 1″ to 2″ pieces

1/2 cup carrots, grated

1/3 cup red cabbage, finely shredded

Makes 5 to 6 cups salad greens.

Pickled Cabbage

Combine the following in a bowl:

2/3 cup cabbage, finely shredded

1/3 cup carrots, grated

1 tablespoon white wine vinegar

2 teaspoons sugar

dash of salt

Allow to marinate in the refrigerator for 24 hours.

Ingredients for Salads continued

Crispy Bean Threads

Crispy bean threads are often tossed into Chinese Chicken Salads. They add a crunchy texture to the salad and help absorb the flavor of the dressing.

Heat oil to 375°. Take a small handful of bean thread noodles and carefully drop into oil. Within seconds they will expand and puff up. Remove from oil and drain.

Crispy Noodles

4 won ton skins, cut into ¼″ wide strips

Fry in oil heated to 350° for 2 to 3 minutes or until golden brown.

Plum Sauce Dressing

Combine the following in a bowl:

    4 tablespoons hoisin sauce

    2 tablespoons plum sauce

  1½ tablespoons white wine vinegar

    2 teaspoons rice wine

    2 teaspoons sesame oil

    1 teaspoon ketchup

Sesame Peanut Dressing

Combine the following in a bowl:

  ⅓ cup white wine vinegar

  2 tablespoons peanut butter, chunky-style

  2 tablespoons brown sugar

  1 tablespoon soy sauce

  2 teaspoons sesame oil

 ¼ teaspoon ground ginger

 ½ teaspoon sesame seeds, toasted

Tibetan Temple

9 Shiitake mushrooms, approximately 1½″ diameter,
soaked in water for 20 minutes to soften. Cut off
the stems and squeeze out excess liquid.

To braise: ⅓ cup vegetable broth

dash ground ginger

dash garlic powder

dash white pepper

Heat ingredients to boiling and add mushrooms. Turn the heat to low and
simmer for 10 minutes. Squeeze out excess liquid.

To fry: 3 tablespoons *Batter Mix* (recipe on page 136)

cornstarch for coating

oil for frying

In a bowl, coat mushrooms with cornstarch. Add the batter mix. Heat
1½″ of oil to 350° and fry mushrooms for 2 to 3 minutes.

5 to 6 cups mixed salad greens

⅔ cup *Pickled Cabbage* (page 112)

small handful of *Crispy Bean Threads* (page 113)

small handful of *Crispy Noodles* (page 113)

½ – ⅔ cup *Plum Sauce Dressing* (page 113)

⅓ cup cashews, roasted

⅓ teaspoon sesame seeds, toasted

After frying mushrooms, cut them into strips approximately ½″ wide.
In a large bowl combine the mushrooms, pickled cabbage, salad greens,
bean threads and crispy noodles. Toss with plum sauce dressing. Arrange
in a large salad bowl and sprinkle with cashews and sesame seeds.
Pictured on page 72.

Cantonese Tofu Salad

2 *Marinated Tofu Cakes* (page 81), cut into ¼″ slices
5 to 6 cups mixed salad greens
     small handful of *Crispy Noodles* (page 113)
     small handful of *Crispy Bean Threads* (page 113)
1 tablespoon peanuts, crushed
½ – ⅔ cup *Sesame Peanut Dressing* (page 113)
¼ cup peanuts, roasted

In a large bowl, toss all ingredients, except roasted peanuts. Arrange in a serving bowl topped with peanuts.

Mediterranean Magic

6 *Tofu Balls* (recipe on page 97)
3 to 4 cups mixed salad greens
½ cup *Pickled Cabbage* (page 112)
1 tomato, cut into half circles
6 spinach leaves

Dressing: Mix the following together:

⅓ cup *Sesame Peanut Dressing* (page 113)
1 teaspoon Tahini Sesame Paste
2 teaspoons white wine vinegar

Place pickled cabbage on the bottom of a serving platter and salad greens over it. Top with tofu balls and drizzle the dressing over all. Garnish with tomatoes and spinach leaves around the perimeter of the platter. *Pictured on page 72.*

115

Early Spring Chicken Salad

8 oz. *Marinated Breast of Chicken* (page 82),
   sliced in half across the middle so it is less thick

5 to 6 cups mixed salad greens

²/₃ cup *Pickled Cabbage* (page 112)
   small handful of *Crispy Noodles* (page 113)
   small handful of *Crispy Bean Threads* (page 113)

¹/₂ – ²/₃ cup *Plum Sauce Dressing* (page 113)

¹/₃ cup cashews, roasted

¹/₃ teaspoon sesame seeds, toasted

2 teaspoons vegetable oil

Pan fry chicken breast in oil over medium-high heat for 4 to 5 minutes or until chicken is cooked through. Cut into ¹/₄″ wide strips. In a large bowl, combine chicken, salad greens, pickled cabbage, crispy noodles and crispy bean threads. Toss with plum sauce dressing. Arrange in a serving bowl topped with cashews and sesame seeds. *Pictured on page 78.*

Cantonese Chicken Salad

8 oz. *Marinated Breast of Chicken* (page 82),
   sliced in half across the middle so it is less thick

5 to 6 cups mixed salad greens

   small handful of *Crispy Noodles* (page 113)

   small handful of *Crispy Bean Threads* (page 113)

2 teaspoons vegetable oil

1 tablespoon crushed peanuts

$\frac{1}{2}$ – $\frac{2}{3}$ cup *Sesame Peanut Dressing* (page 113)

$\frac{1}{4}$ cup roasted peanuts

In a skillet, heat oil and pan-fry chicken over medium-high heat for
4 to 5 minutes or until chicken is cooked through. Cut chicken into $\frac{1}{4}''$ wide
strips. In a large bowl, toss chicken strips, salad greens, crispy noodles,
crispy bean threads, crushed peanuts and dressing. Arrange in a large
serving bowl topped with roasted peanuts.

Sea of Paradise

9 *Marinated Prawns* (page 83), approximately 3.5 oz.

3 to 4 cups *Mixed Salad Greens* (page 112)

¹/₂ cup *Pickled Cabbage* (page 112)

Honey Mustard Dressing

seasonal fruit, sliced

Glazed Walnuts

Glazed Walnuts

¹/₃ cup walnuts   2 teaspoons honey

Bake walnuts in a pre-heated oven at 350° for 25 minutes. Remove from oven and coat walnuts with honey. Return to oven for an additional 1 to 2 minutes.

Drop prawns in boiling water and turn down heat slightly, Cook prawns for 3 minutes. Remove them with a slotted spoon and rinse in cold water.

On a serving platter, arrange Pickled Cabbage with Salad Greens on top. Garnish the perimeter of the plate with sliced seasonal fruit. Mix prawns with the Honey Mustard Dressing and arrange on top of greens. Sprinkle with the glazed walnuts. *Pictured on page 72.*

Honey Mustard Dressing

Combine the following ingredients in a bowl:

3 tablespoons mayonnaise

2 teaspoons Dijon mustard

1 teaspoon yellow mustard

1 teaspoon honey

dash of worcestershire sauce

Autumn Harvest

8 snow pea pods

8 zucchini pieces, sliced

8 carrot pieces, thinly sliced

4 broccoli flowerets

4 cauliflower flowerets

4 button mushrooms, halved

4 pieces canned baby corn (available in the Asian section)

¼ cup celery, sliced diagonally ¼″ thick

2 teaspoons vegetable oil

2 teaspoons black bean sauce

2 teaspoons rice wine

1 teaspoon garlic, minced

1 cup vegetable broth

⅓ cup cashews, roasted

Place a skillet or wok over high heat. Add oil. When oil is hot, add garlic and black bean sauce and sauté for a few seconds. Add cauliflower and broccoli and sauté with wine for 1 minute. Add broth and remaining vegetables and cook for 5 to 6 minutes or until vegetables soften. Sprinkle cashews on top and remove from heat.

Bag of Fortune ☯ Vegetarian

 2 Marinated Tofu Cakes (page 81), cut into 1″ cubes

¾ cup button mushrooms, halved if large

¾ cup zucchini, thinly sliced

⅔ cup water chestnuts

⅓ cup carrots, thinly sliced

 2 teaspoons vegetable oil

 2 teaspoons rice wine

 1 teaspoon garlic, minced

 1 teaspoon ginger, minced

 1 teaspoon soy sauce

⅔ cup vegetable broth

½ teaspoon salt

 1 teaspoon fresh basil, finely chopped

 1 teaspoon hoisin sauce

¼ teaspoon chili sauce

    Cornstarch solution: 1 teaspoon cornstarch
    mixed with 2 teaspoons water

 1 flour tortilla, 12″ diameter,
    steamed until softened

 1 green onion, blanched,
    white part of onion removed

 1 piece of string

 8 broccoli flowerets,
    steamed and set aside

 4 carrot pieces, thinly sliced,
    steamed and set aside

Bag of Fortune ☯ Vegetarian continued

Place skillet or wok over high heat. Add oil. When the oil is hot, add garlic and ginger and sauté for a few seconds. Add tofu, wine and soy sauce and sauté for 1 minute. Add remaining vegetables, broth and salt. Cook for 5 minutes. Stir in hoisin sauce and chili sauce. Add fresh basil. Stir in the cornstarch solution to seal in the flavor of the sauces.

Allow tortilla wrap and filling to cool before assembling. Put filling in center of tortilla and tie into a sack with string. Fry in oil heated to 350° for about 5 minutes or until golden brown. Remove from heat and allow to drain on paper towels. (You can also bake the Bag of Fortune in an oven preheated to 350° for 35 to 40 minutes.) Arrange the Bag of Fortune in the center of a plate. Cut the string and tie with green onion. Garnish with steamed broccoli and carrots around perimeter. *Pictured on page 73.*

Bag of Fortune Chicken

Follow the same procedure but replace the Vegetarian filling with *Four Seasons Chicken* (recipe on page 139).

Buddha's Delight

2 *Marinated Tofu Cakes* (page 81), cut into ½″ cubes
1 cup zucchini, cut into ½″ cubes
1 cup broccoli, cut into 1″ pieces
½ cup button mushrooms, quartered
⅓ cup peas and diced carrots, combined
⅓ cup *BBQ Soy Protein* (page 84), cut into ½″ pieces
2 teaspoons vegetable oil
1 teaspoon garlic, minced
1 teaspoon soy sauce
1 teaspoon rice wine
1 cup vegetable broth
1 teaspoon Shiitake mushroom sauce
⅛ teaspoon white pepper

Place skillet or wok over high heat. Add oil. When the oil is hot, add garlic and sauté for a few seconds to release flavor. Add all vegetables except the soy protein. Stir in soy sauce and rice wine and sauté for 2 minutes. Add vegetable broth and cover for 3 minutes over medium heat. Remove cover and add soy protein and mushroom sauce. Stir until well blended. Season with white pepper.

Cupid's Delight

2   *Marinated Tofu Cakes* (page 81), sliced across
     the middle so it is less thick
2   teaspoons vegetable oil
1   teaspoon garlic, minced
1   teaspoon rice wine
½   cup zucchini, finely chopped
½   cup button mushrooms, finely chopped
¼   cup tomatoes, finely chopped
3   tablespoons marinara sauce*
½   cup cheddar and Jack cheese combined, shredded
2   teaspoons fresh basil, finely chopped
     radish rose petals
     3″ heart-shaped cookie cutter

Cut the tofu into 4 heart-shaped pieces. (Save the scraps for pot stickers or won tons.) Warm in the oven. Meanwhile, heat oil in a skillet. Add garlic and sauté zucchini and mushrooms with wine. After 1 minute, add tomatoes. Stir in marinara sauce and sauté for 2 minutes. Sprinkle with cheese and cook until it melts.

To assemble, put 2 tofu halves on a plate. Add cheese filling on top. Sprinkle with fresh basil. Arrange remaining tofu halves on top to form a sandwich. Because the cheese filling tends to overflow, an alternate method is to put the cheese filling on a plate and the 4 heart-shaped tofu on top with the points going toward the center to form a four-leaf clover. Garnish with radish rose petals. *Pictured on page 73.*

* At Joy Meadow we make our own marinara sauce from scratch, but the quantity is too large and the process too time-consuming for the small amount required. There are many wonderful tomato and marinara sauces available in the marketplace that you can use for this recipe.

Enchanted Forest

2 *Marinated Tofu Cakes* (page 81), cut into ¼″ slices
2 teaspoons vegetable oil
½ teaspoon garlic, minced
8 broccoli flowerets
8 cauliflower flowerets
  salt and pepper to taste
  Plum Sauce mixture

Cook broccoli and cauliflower in boiling water until tender, approximately 4 minutes. Drain out water and season to taste with salt and pepper. Arrange around the perimeter of a platter, alternating between broccoli and cauliflower.

Place a wide skillet over medium-high heat. Add oil. When hot, add garlic and sauté for a few seconds to release flavor. Add tofu slices and cook for approximately 3 minutes, turning over to heat both sides. Pour in sauce and cook for an additional 1 minute, turning the tofu over as it browns (plum sauce will burn if cooked too long). Remove from heat. Place tofu slices in the center of the prepared platter.

Plum Sauce Mixture

Combine the following ingredients in a small bowl until blended:

  2 teaspoons hoisin sauce

  1 teaspoon plum sauce

  1 teaspoon water

  ½ teaspoon ketchup

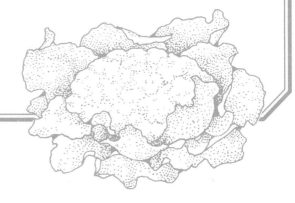

Farmer's Bouquet

8 *Marinated Tofu* pieces (page 81), cut into 1″ cubes

8 bell pepper pieces, cut into 1″ squares

8 zucchini pieces, sliced

8 button mushrooms

8 cherry tomatoes

Hoisin Mustard Marinade

2 cups cooked brown rice

4 skewers

Thread 2-each of the vegetables onto the 4 skewers. Place the vegetable skewers on a baking dish and brush generously with the Hoisin Mustard Marinade. Broil for 10 minutes. Turn the skewers midway through to ensure even cooking. Pile the brown rice on a large serving platter and arrange the vegetable skewers on top. Pour the remaining marinade sauce from the baking dish over the skewers and rice. *Pictured on page 73.*

Hoisin Mustard Marinade

4 tablespoons hoisin sauce

2 tablespoons plum sauce

2 teaspoons rice wine

2 teaspoons white wine vinegar

1 teaspoon ketchup

1 teaspoon honey

1 teaspoon sesame oil

1 teaspoon Chinese hot mustard

Golden Chalice

7 oz. Chinese eggplant*

1 *Nepal Loaf* slice (page 130), cooked

Marinara sauce, white sauce or shredded cheese

Cut the eggplant in half lengthwise. Scoop out the flesh and finely chop. Mix the chopped eggplant flesh with the Nepal Loaf. Mound the filling into the eggplant halves. Bake in a preheated oven at 350° for approximately 40 minutes or until the tops are golden brown and the eggplant is tender. Top with your favorite marinara sauce, white sauce or a generous sprinkling of cheese. *Pictured on page 73.*

*   *Use the smaller Chinese eggplant for this recipe. If you use the larger American variety you will need to salt, rinse and drain the eggplant first in order to release the bitter taste.*

Lotus Blossom

2 *Marinated Tofu Cakes* (page 81), cut into ¼″ cubes
⅔ cup celery, finely chopped
⅔ cup zucchini, finely chopped
⅔ cup button mushrooms, finely chopped
½ cup water chestnuts, finely chopped
½ cup onions, finely chopped
¼ cup snow peas, finely chopped
¼ cup carrots, finely chopped
2 teaspoons vegetable oil
1 teaspoon garlic, minced
1 teaspoon rice wine
1 teaspoon soy sauce
¼ teaspoon salt
1 tablespoon brown bean sauce
   (the brand that isn't spicy)
¼ teaspoon sesame oil
1 tablespoon roasted peanuts, crushed

Place a wide skillet or wok over high heat. When skillet is hot, add oil. When oil heats up, sauté garlic for a few seconds to release flavor. Add onions and tofu. Sauté with wine and soy sauce for 2 minutes. Add remaining vegetables and salt and sauté for 3 to 4 minutes. Stir in brown bean sauce until well blended. Add crushed peanuts. Season with sesame oil. Remove from heat and serve on top of a large lettuce leaf.

Have a plate of additional lettuce leaves for wrapping and 1 tablespoon of hoisin sauce. To eat, put a dollop of hoisin sauce and a tablespoon of Lotus Blossom filling on a lettuce leaf, wrap and enjoy! *Pictured on page 74.*

Midsummer Night's Dream

Combine the following ingredients in a bowl:

$1/2$ cup walnuts, finely chopped

$1/2$ cup celery, finely chopped

$1/4$ cup water chestnuts, finely chopped

$1/4$ cup onions, finely chopped

$1/4$ cup carrots, finely chopped

1 teaspoon fresh cilantro, finely chopped

$1/2$ teaspoon salt

$1/4$ teaspoon ground ginger

$1/4$ teaspoon garlic powder

$1/4$ teaspoon 5-spice powder

Add the following and mix well:

1 tablespoon all-purpose flour

1 tablespoon cornstarch

1 tablespoon glutinous rice flour

With well-floured hands, form mixture into croquettes. Roll in additional cornstarch before frying. Heat 2″ of vegetable oil to 350°. Carefully drop croquettes into hot oil and fry for approximately 6 minutes. Remove from oil and drain on paper towels.
Makes 8 to 10 croquettes.

Midsummer Night's Dream *continued*

Boil the following vegetables in water for 1 minute, then drain and set aside:

$\frac{1}{4}$ cup bell pepper, cut into 1″ squares

$\frac{1}{4}$ cup carrots, thinly sliced

$\frac{1}{4}$ cup onions, cut into 1″ squares

$\frac{1}{4}$ cup celery, sliced diagonally $\frac{1}{4}$″ thick

$\frac{1}{2}$ teaspoon sesame oil

1 recipe *Tangy Spicy Sauce*

In a skillet, heat Tangy Spicy Sauce. When sauce begins to boil add vegetables and croquettes. Sprinkle with sesame oil. If croquettes were prepared ahead of time, put them in the oven to warm first. *Pictured on page 74.*

Tangy Spicy Sauce

Combine the following ingredients in a small bowl until blended:

$\frac{1}{3}$ cup ketchup

$\frac{1}{4}$ cup red wine vinegar

$\frac{1}{4}$ cup brown sugar, packed

$\frac{1}{4}$ teaspoon chili garlic sauce

Nepal Loaf

Combine the following ingredients in a mixing bowl:

    1 cup cooked brown rice (cooked in water with no seasoning)

    ²/₃ cup *Marinated Tofu* (page 81), finely chopped

    ²/₃ cup celery, finely chopped

    ¹/₄ cup onions, finely chopped

    ¹/₄ cup water chestnuts, finely chopped

    ¹/₄ cup carrots, finely chopped

    ²/₃ teaspoon salt

    ¹/₂ teaspoon garlic powder

    ¹/₂ teaspoon dried basil

    ¹/₄ teaspoon dried oregano

    ¹/₄ teaspoon white pepper

In a small bowl combine:

    1 tablespoon cornstarch

    mixed with 2 tablespoons water

Mix the cornstarch solution with the vegetables and seasonings to bind ingredients. Brush an 8″ × 8″ baking pan with olive oil. Press the mixture into the pan and bake in a 350° preheated oven for 40 minutes. Cut into 4 slices and serve with mushroom gravy and seasonal vegetables. *Pictured on page 74.*

Mushroom Gravy

²/₃ cup vegetable broth

¹/₈ cup button mushrooms, sliced

2 teaspoons Shiitake mushroom sauce

Cornstarch solution:

1 teaspoon cornstarch mixed with 2 teaspoons water

Heat broth until boiling. Add mushrooms and mushroom sauce. To thicken, stir in cornstarch solution. Pour in a gravy boat and serve with *Nepal Loaf.*

Panda's Village

1½ cups taro root, cut into slices and boiled
    in water for 15 minutes, then drained

  1 tablespoon cornstarch

  1 tablespoon dry bread crumbs

  ¼ teaspoon salt

10 pieces of canned sliced bamboo shoots
    (bamboo shoots approximately 2″ long by ½″ wide)

    additional cornstarch for coating

Mash the cooked taro root then mix with cornstarch and bread crumbs until it resembles stiff mashed potatoes. Divide the taro root mixture into 10 portions approximately 1½″ round. Flatten the taro root balls. Put 1 piece of bamboo shoot inside, leaving ½″ protruding to resemble a sparerib bone. Fold taro over to close. Roll in cornstarch. Put 2″ of oil in a pan or wok and heat to 350°. Fry taro root for 5 minutes or until crispy on the outside. Drain and arrange on a serving platter. *Pictured on page 74.*

Savory Sweet Sauce

Combine the following ingredients in a bowl:

  ½ cup water

  3 tablespoons brown sugar

1½ tablespoons white wine vinegar

  1 teaspoon Shiitake mushroom sauce

  ¼ teaspoon chili garlic sauce

    Cornstarch solution: 1 teaspoon
    cornstarch mixed with 2 teaspoons water

Heat the sauce in a pan until it boils, then thicken with cornstarch solution. Pour sauce over "spareribs." Serve with steamed snow peas, sliced carrots and zucchini.

Tofu Foo Yung

Combine the following ingredients in a large bowl:

2 *Marinated Tofu Cakes* (page 81), cut into ¼" cubes
⅓ cup celery, finely chopped
⅓ cup cabbage, finely chopped
¼ cup button mushrooms, finely chopped
¼ cup bean sprouts, finely chopped
⅛ cup snow peas, finely chopped
⅛ cup carrots, finely chopped
⅛ cup onions, finely chopped
1 tablespoon cornstarch
½ teaspoon salt
⅛ teaspoon white pepper
2 eggs, beaten

Heat a wide skillet over medium-high heat. Add 3 tablespoons vegetable oil. With a ladle, scoop the tofu-egg mixture into the skillet forming 4 patties, 3" to 4" in diameter. Cook over medium heat until brown on one side, approximately 2 to 3 minutes. Flip tofu-egg patties over, reduce heat to low and cook an additional 3 to 4 minutes or until eggs are set and patties are firm. Remove from heat and arrange on a platter.

Tofu Foo Yung Gravy

⅔ cup vegetable broth
⅛ cup button mushrooms, sliced
2 teaspoons Shiitake mushroom sauce

Cornstarch solution:
1 teaspoon cornstarch mixed with 2 teaspoons water

Heat broth until boiling. Add mushrooms and mushroom sauce. To thicken, stir in cornstarch solution. Pour sauce over *Tofu Foo Yung*.

Winter Into Spring

1½ cups *BBQ Soy Protein* (page 84)

1½ cups *Crispy Bean Threads* (page 113)

1 cup zucchini, julienned and cut 4″ long

⅔ cup carrots, julienned and cut 4″ long

4 slices cucumber, cut in half to make semi-circles

2 teaspoons vegetable oil, divided

1 teaspoon rice wine

½ teaspoon garlic, minced

¼ teaspoon salt

1 tablespoon water

plum sauce mixture

Plum Sauce Mixture

Combine the following ingredients in a bowl:

4 teaspoons hoisin sauce

2 teaspoons plum sauce

1 teaspoon ketchup

Arrange bean threads on a serving platter to resemble a bed of "snow." Heat a skillet or wok over high heat, adding 1 teaspoon of oil when hot. When oil heats up, add garlic and sauté for a few seconds. Add the vegetables and salt and sauté for 3 minutes. Pour the vegetables over the bean thread "snow."

In the same skillet, add the remaining 1 teaspoon of oil. When hot, sauté the soy protein. Stir soy protein with water until heated through. Stir in the plum sauce mixture until soy protein is evenly coated. (If plum sauce is cooked too long, it tends to burn.) Remove from heat and pour on top of sautéed vegetables and "snow." Arrange sliced cucumbers around perimeter. If you have organic flowers, garnish the "snow" with a few petals to represent the first sign of Spring after Winter. *Pictured on page 75.*

Zen Banquet

2 heaping cups of potatoes, cut into 1″ chunks

½ teaspoon salt

½ teaspoon garlic powder

3 tablespoons cornstarch

6 tablespoons vegetarian won ton filling
(see *Yin Yang Delight*, page 91)
oil for frying

Boil potatoes until softened. Drain and allow to cool. In a large bowl mix potatoes, salt and garlic powder. Knead until potatoes resemble dough. (Our chefs wear surgical gloves to prevent the potatoes from sticking to their hands.) Add the cornstarch as you knead. Form the potatoes into 3″ balls, then into the shape of a bowl. Place 1 tablespoon of filling inside the "potato bowl." Enclose the filling, forming a pear shape as you go. Roll in cornstarch. Heat oil to 350°. Fry "pears" for 3 minutes. Remove from heat and allow to cool for a few minutes. Return to oil and fry an additional 2 minutes or until golden brown. (If you fry "pears" for 5 consecutive minutes, the potatoes will sometimes burst from the heat.) Remove "pears" from oil and allow to drain on paper towels. Pierce tops with a toothpick and insert a stem of parsley to resemble the stem of a pear. Makes 6.

Serve with a side of *Plum Sauce Vegetables* (next page) and additional plum sauce for dipping.

Plum Sauce Mixture

Combine the following ingredients in a bowl and set aside:

2 tablespoons hoisin sauce

1 tablespoon plum sauce

1 teaspoon ketchup

1 tablespoon water

Zen Banquet *continued*

Plum Sauce Vegetables

²/₃ cup vegetable broth

²/₃ cup zucchini, sliced

¹/₂ cup carrots, sliced

¹/₂ cup mushrooms, sliced

1 tablespoon Plum Sauce Mixture

In a skillet, heat broth. When it starts to boil, add vegetables and cook for 3 to 4 minutes. Stir in 1 tablespoon of plum sauce mixture. Put the remaining plum sauce mixture in a dipping bowl. Arrange the "pears" on 2 platters with plum sauce vegetables and small bowl of dipping sauce. *Pictured on page 75.*

Ambrosia

10 oz. boneless breast of chicken, sliced in half
across the middle so it's less thick

Marinade

1 teaspoon soy sauce

1 teaspoon lemon juice

1 teaspoon rice wine

1 teaspoon sesame oil

½ teaspoon salt

½ teaspoon ginger, minced

½ teaspoon lemon peel, grated

½ teaspoon cornstarch

⅛ teaspoon white pepper

In a bowl, combine the ingredients for the marinade. Thoroughly
coat the chicken breast in the marinade and let stand for 15 minutes.

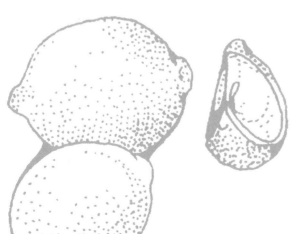

Batter Mix

¼ cup all-purpose flour

¼ cup water

1 egg

2 tablespoons cornstarch

½ teaspoon salt

¼ teaspoon baking powder

In a bowl, mix the batter ingredients until smooth.
Dip the chicken breast into the batter until evenly coated.

Ambrosia (continued)

In a skillet or wok, heat 1½″ of vegetable oil to 360°. Carefully drop chicken breast into oil and fry for approximately 6 minutes, turning over as needed. Remove from heat and drain on paper towels.

Lemon Sauce

Combine the first 5 ingredients in a small bowl until blended:

- ½ cup water
- ¼ cup lemon juice
- ¼ cup honey
- 2 teaspoons plum sauce
- ½ teaspoon grated lemon peel (optional)
  Cornstarch solution: 1 teaspoon cornstarch mixed with 2 teaspoons water

---

In a skillet, heat the Lemon Sauce until boiling. Thicken with cornstarch solution. Slice the chicken breast crosswise about 2/3″ wide and arrange on a platter. Pour the lemon sauce on top. Serve with seasonal vegetables and rice. *Pictured on page 75.*

Empress Chicken

8 oz. *Marinated Breast of Chicken* (page 82),
cut into bite-size pieces

2 teaspoons vegetable oil

2 teaspoons rice wine

1 teaspoon garlic, minced

$\frac{1}{3}$ cup onions, cut into 1″ squares

1 teaspoon soy sauce

$\frac{1}{2}$ cup vegetable or chicken broth

$\frac{2}{3}$ teaspoon salt

$\frac{1}{3}$ cup cashews, roasted

Cornstarch solution: 1 teaspoon cornstarch
mixed with 2 teaspoons water

Boil following vegetables in water for 2 minutes, then drain in a colander:

8 zucchini pieces, thinly sliced

8 carrot pieces, thinly sliced

8 snow pea pods

6 broccoli flowerets

4 button mushrooms, halved

$\frac{1}{4}$ cup celery, sliced diagonally $\frac{1}{4}$″ thick

Place a skillet or wok over high heat. Add oil when hot. When oil heats up, add garlic and onions and sauté for 20 to 30 seconds. Add chicken, soy sauce and wine. Sauté for 2 minutes to brown chicken. Stir in vegetables, broth and salt. After sautéing for 3 to 4 minutes, stir in the cornstarch solution to bind the seasonings. Sprinkle with cashews.

Four Seasons Chicken

8 oz. *Marinated Breast of Chicken* (page 82),
       cut into bite-size pieces
    2 teaspoons vegetable oil
    1 teaspoon garlic, minced
    2 slices fresh ginger
    2 teaspoons rice wine
    1 teaspoon soy sauce
 ½ cup vegetable or chicken broth
    2 teaspoons hoisin sauce
 ¼ teaspoon Chinese chili sauce
    1 teaspoon fresh basil, finely chopped

Boil following vegetables in water for 2 minutes, then drain in a colander:

    8 broccoli flowerets
    8 zucchini pieces, thinly sliced
    8 carrot pieces, thinly sliced
    4 pieces canned baby corn (available in the Asian section)

Place a skillet or wok over high heat. When hot, add oil. When oil
heats up, add garlic and ginger and sauté for a few seconds. Add chicken,
soy sauce and wine. Brown the chicken for 2 minutes. Add vegetables
and broth and sauté 3 minutes. Add hoisin sauce, chili sauce and basil.
Stir in the cornstarch solution to seal in the flavor of the sauces.
Pictured on page 75.

Five Happiness Chicken

8 oz. *Marinated Breast of Chicken* (page 82),
    cut into bite-size pieces
2 teaspoons vegetable oil
2 teaspoons rice wine
1 teaspoon soy sauce
1 teaspoon garlic, minced
1/3 cup onions, cut into 1″ squares
1/2 cup vegetable or chicken broth
1/8 cup green peas
1 teaspoon chili garlic sauce
1/4 cup roasted peanuts
1/4 teaspoon sesame oil
1/3 teaspoon toasted sesame seeds
    Cornstarch solution: 1 teaspoon cornstarch
    mixed with 2 teaspoons water

Boil following vegetables in water for 1 minute, then drain in a colander:

1/3 cup bell peppers, cut into 1″ squares
1/3 cup celery, sliced diagonally 1/4″ thick
1/3 cup zucchini, thinly sliced
1/4 cup carrots, thinly sliced

In a hot skillet or wok sauté garlic and onions for 20 to 30 seconds. Add chicken, wine and soy sauce. Brown the chicken for 2 minutes. Add broth, green peas and vegetables and sauté for 3 minutes. Stir in chili sauce until well blended. Add peanuts and sesame oil. Stir in the cornstarch solution to bind the seasonings. Arrange on a serving platter and sprinkle with sesame seeds.

General Tso's Chicken

8 oz. *Marinated Breast of Chicken* (page 82),
    cut into bite-size pieces
    Batter Mix (recipe on page 136)
    oil for frying
½ teaspoon garlic, minced

Boil following vegetables in water for 1 minute, then drain in a colander:

    ½ cup zucchini, thinly sliced
    ½ cup button mushrooms, halved
    ¼ cup carrots, thinly sliced

Coat the chicken in batter mix. Fry in oil heated to 350° for 3 minutes or until chicken is cooked through. Remove with a slotted spoon and drain.

In a wide skillet, heat the garlic and the General Tso Sauce. When the mixture starts to boil add vegetables. Sauté for 1 minute before adding fried chicken pieces. Stir until chicken is well coated.

General Tso Sauce

Mix the following ingredients in a bowl:

    ½ cup water
    3 tablespoons brown sugar, packed
    1½ tablespoons white wine vinegar
    1 teaspoon oyster sauce
    ¼ teaspoon chili garlic sauce

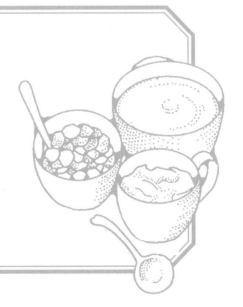

Jade Palace Chicken

Boil following vegetables in water for 3 to 4 minutes, then drain in a colander:

8 broccoli flowerets

8 cauliflower flowerets

1 teaspoon vegetable oil

½ teaspoon garlic, minced

½ teaspoon salt

Heat a skillet with oil. When hot add garlic and sauté for a few seconds. Add broccoli, cauliflower and salt. Stir fry for 30 seconds. Arrange on a platter alternating between broccoli and cauliflower around perimeter of plate.

8 oz. *Marinated Breast of Chicken* (page 82),

cut into bite-size pieces

2 teaspoons vegetable oil

1 teaspoon garlic, minced

Plum Sauce Mixture

Combine the following ingredients in a bowl:

2 teaspoons hoisin sauce

1 teaspoon plum sauce

½ teaspoon ketchup

1 teaspoon water

Heat a skillet with oil. When hot add garlic and sauté for a few seconds. Add chicken and cook over medium-high heat for 3 to 4 minutes. Stir in plum sauce mixture until chicken is well-coated. (If plum sauce is cooked too long it can burn.) Arrange the chicken in the center of the prepared broccoli and cauliflower platter.

Starfire Chicken

8 oz. *Marinated Breast of Chicken* (page 82),
  cut into bite-size pieces

2 teaspoons vegetable oil

2 teaspoons rice wine

1 teaspoon garlic, minced

⅓ cup onions, cut into 1″ squares

½ cup *Tangy Spicy Sauce* (page 129)
  mixed with a dash of worcestershire sauce

Boil following vegetables in water for 1 minute, then drain in a colander:

⅓ cup bell peppers, cut into 1″ squares

⅓ cup carrots, thinly sliced

⅓ cup zucchini, thinly sliced

⅓ cup celery, sliced diagonally ¼″ thick

Heat skillet with oil. When hot sauté garlic and onions for 20 to 30 seconds. Add chicken and stir-fry with wine for 2 to 3 minutes over medium-high heat. Stir in vegetables and Tangy Spicy Sauce and cook for 2 to 3 more minutes or until chicken is cooked through.

East Meets West

8 oz. linguini, cooked *al dente*

4 *Marinated Prawns* (page 83)

5 oz. *Marinated Breast of Chicken* (page 82),
cut into bite-size pieces

2 teaspoons vegetable oil

1 teaspoon garlic, minced

1 teaspoon rice wine

½ teaspoon soy sauce

⅔ cup vegetable or chicken broth

½ teaspoon oyster sauce

⅛ teaspoon white pepper

Cornstarch solution: 1 teaspoon cornstarch
mixed with 2 teaspoons water

Boil the prawns and the following vegetables in water for 1½ minutes, then drain in a colander:

¾ cup Napa cabbage, cut into 2″ squares

6 broccoli flowerets

6 snow pea pods

6 pieces zucchini, thinly sliced

6 pieces carrot, thinly sliced

3 button mushrooms, halved

3 pieces Shiitake mushrooms

Meanwhile, in a hot skillet or wok add oil. When hot, add garlic and sauté for a few seconds. Add chicken, soy sauce and wine. Brown chicken for 1 to 2 minutes. Add the prawns, vegetables and broth. Sauté for 3 to 4 minutes. Stir in the oyster sauce. To seal the flavors, add the cornstarch solution. Season with white pepper. Arrange linguini on a large platter and pour sautéed chicken, prawns and vegetables on top. *Pictured on page 76.*

Cape Cod Fantasy

9 oz. calamari, washed and drained. Pat dry.

Marinate calamari for 15 minutes in the following ingredients:

$^2/_3$ teaspoons vegetable oil

$^2/_3$ teaspoon cornstarch

$^2/_3$ teaspoon salt

$^1/_2$ teaspoon rice wine

$^1/_6$ teaspoon white pepper

additional cornstarch for coating

Batter Mix (page 136)

oil for frying

In a bowl coat calamari with cornstarch. Add batter mix. Heat 2″ of oil to 350° and fry calamari for 4 to 5 minutes. Remove and drain. Arrange on a platter with lemon wedges and plum sauce for dipping. Serve with *Baked Potato Cake* (page 83) and seasonal vegetables. *Pictured on page 76.*

Seashore Surprise

5 oz. calamari steak, washed and drained. Pat dry.

Marinate calamari for 15 minutes in the following ingredients:

$\frac{1}{4}$ teaspoon salt

$\frac{1}{4}$ teaspoon rice wine

$\frac{1}{4}$ teaspoon water

$\frac{1}{8}$ teaspoon baking soda

$\frac{1}{8}$ teaspoon white pepper

1 tablespoon vegetable oil

  all-purpose flour for coating

$\frac{1}{8}$ teaspoon white pepper

1 teaspoon lemon, including peel, chopped

1 teaspoon rice wine

1 teaspoon lemon juice

$\frac{1}{2}$ teaspoon capers

$\frac{1}{4}$ teaspoon garlic, minced

$\frac{1}{4}$ cup vegetable or chicken broth

  Cornstarch solution: $\frac{1}{2}$ teaspoon cornstarch

mixed with 1 teaspoon water

Coat calamari with flour. Put oil in a skillet and pan fry calamari over medium-high heat for 2 minutes, flipping over as it turns golden yellow. Sprinkle with white pepper and cook the other side on medium heat for 2 minutes or until cooked through. Remove from skillet and arrange on a serving plate. In the same skillet add garlic, chopped lemon, wine and capers and sauté for a few seconds before adding broth and lemon juice. Cook until the mixture boils. Add cornstarch solution to thicken sauce. Pour sauce over calamari steak. Serve with seasonal vegetables and *Baked Potato Cake* (page 83).

Emerald Garden Prawns

14 *Marinated Prawns* (page 82)

2 teaspoons vegetable oil

1 teaspoon garlic, minced

2 teaspoons rice wine

$\frac{2}{3}$ cup vegetable or chicken broth

$\frac{1}{2}$ teaspoon oyster sauce

$\frac{1}{8}$ teaspoon white pepper

Cornstarch solution: 1 teaspoon cornstarch
mixed with 2 teaspoons water

Boil the following vegetables in water for 2 minutes, then drain in a colander:

8 pieces zucchini, thinly sliced

8 pieces carrot, thinly sliced

8 snow pea pods

4 broccoli flowerets

4 cauliflower flowerets

4 button mushrooms, halved

In a hot skillet or wok heat oil. When hot, add garlic and sauté for a few seconds. Add prawns and wine and sauté over medium-high heat for 1 minute. Add vegetables and broth and cook for 3 to 4 minutes. Stir in the oyster sauce. Seal in the flavors by adding the cornstarch solution. Season with white pepper.

Neptune's Dream

14 *Marinated Prawns* (page 82)

2 teaspoons vegetable oil

1 teaspoon garlic, minced

2 teaspoons tomatoes, finely chopped

2 teaspoons rice wine

1 teaspoon green onions, finely chopped

Neptune's Dream Sauce

Steam the following vegetables for 4 minutes. Season with salt and pepper:

8 broccoli flowerets

8 pieces carrot, thinly sliced

8 pieces zucchini, thinly sliced

In a hot skillet heat oil. When hot, add garlic and tomatoes. Stir in prawns and cook over medium-high heat for 2 minutes, flipping prawns over as they turn pink. Add wine. Turn heat down to low and stir Neptune's Dream Sauce into the prawns. Add green onions. Serve with steamed vegetables. *Pictured on page 76.*

Neptune's Dream Sauce

Mix the following ingredients in a small bowl:

1 $\frac{1}{2}$ tablespoons salted cream butter

1 tablespoons Heinz 57 Sauce

$\frac{1}{2}$ egg yolk

$\frac{1}{8}$ teaspoon black pepper

Pisces Moon

14 *Marinated Prawns* (page 82)
 1 flour tortilla shell
   oil for frying

$\frac{1}{8}$ cup snow peas, julienned
$\frac{1}{8}$ cup carrots, julienned
$\frac{1}{8}$ cup onions, julienned
$\frac{1}{8}$ cup celery, thinly sliced
$\frac{1}{8}$ cup Shiitake mushrooms, thinly sliced
$\frac{1}{8}$ cup button mushrooms, thinly sliced
 2 teaspoons vegetable oil
 1 teaspoon rice wine
 1 teaspoon garlic, minced
$\frac{1}{3}$ teaspoon salt
$\frac{1}{3}$ cup *Tangy Spicy Sauce* (recipe on page 129)
   mixed with a dash of worcestershire sauce

In oil heated to 350° fry tortilla shell. With round metal ladle, press on center of tortilla to form a bowl. Hold the ladle for 1 minute until tortilla shell hardens. Remove from oil and drain. Set on a serving platter. To create the same effect without the oil, put tortilla in a round bowl with a smaller bowl to anchor. Microwave for 4 minutes.

In a hot skillet or wok, add oil and sauté garlic and onions for a few seconds. Add remaining vegetables, wine and salt. Sauté 1 to 2 minutes. Pour vegetables on top of prepared tortilla bowl.

In a skillet over medium-high heat, add oil and when the oil is hot sauté prawns for 2 minutes, flipping the prawns over as they turn pink. Turn heat down to medium-low and add Tangy Spicy Sauce. Sauté prawns until they are well-coated and sauce is hot. Pour prawns on top of prepared vegetables and tortilla shell. *Pictured on page 76.*

Midnight Seascapes

4 oz. *Marinated Scallops* (page 151, top), halved if large

3 oz. *Marinated Prawns* (page 83)

  2 teaspoons vegetable oil

  1 teaspoon garlic, minced

  2 teaspoons black bean sauce

  1 teaspoon rice wine

  $2/3$ cup vegetable or chicken broth

  $1/2$ teaspoon oyster sauce

  $1/8$ teaspoon white pepper

  Cornstarch solution: 1 teaspoon cornstarch
mixed with 2 teaspoons water

  $1/3$ cup bell peppers, cut into 1″ squares

  $1/3$ cup onions, cut into 1″ squares

  $1/3$ cup celery, sliced diagonally $1/4$″ thick

  $1/2$ cup zucchini, thinly sliced

In a skillet or wok, heat oil. When hot add garlic, black bean sauce and onions. Sauté for 20 seconds before adding scallops and prawns. Stir-fry for 1 minute with wine. Add vegetables and broth and cook for 3 to 4 minutes. Stir in the oyster sauce. Add the cornstarch solution to seal in the flavors of the sauce. Season with white pepper.

Jewel Sea

5 oz. scallops, washed and drained. If large, cut in half. Pat dry
and marinate in the following ingredients for 15 minutes:

½ teaspoon vegetable oil
½ teaspoon cornstarch
¼ teaspoon salt
¼ teaspoon rice wine
⅛ teaspoon white pepper
additional cornstarch for coating
Batter Mix (recipe on page 134)
oil for frying

In a bowl, coat scallops with cornstarch. Add batter mix and coat
evenly. Heat 2″ of oil to 350° and fry scallops for 4 to 5 minutes.
Remove and drain.

---

cantaloupe
seasonal fruit
⅔ cup *Sweet and Sour Sauce* (recipe on page 84)

With a melon ball cutter, scoop out 1 cup of cantaloupe. Arrange the
melon balls on the bottom of a serving platter. Surround the platter with
seasonal fruit. Place scallops in the
center. Drizzle with Sweet and Sour
Sauce. Serve with *Baked Potato Cake*
(page 85).

Be not forgetful to entertain strangers,
for thereby some have entertained
angels unaware.

— Hebrews 13:2

Angel
Light

Angel Light
Books & Gifts

At **Angel Light Books & Gifts** we believe there are many paths to enlightenment. Peruse our vast selection of metaphysical books from Astrology to Zen. Broaden your horizon with stimulating readings on relationships, gardening and holistic health. Stock up on spiritual tools such as incense, candles, crystals, feng shui items and meditation supplies. Sample our hand-blended massage oils, bath salts and potpourri gathered from herbs and petals in our garden. Select among a myriad of unique gift items including angel figurines, children's literature, hand-painted boxes and jewelry.

Follow the scented path to our Secret Garden. Tucked behind the shop is an enchanted garden where the flower fairies play.

*"The way I see it, if you want the rainbow,
you gotta put up with some rain."*

—Dolly Parton

When I first opened my metaphysical bookstore I named it *Harmony Bookshop*. The logo was an opened book with the Chinese character for *harmony* emblazoned on the page. Eighty percent of my sales comprised of books, with incense, candles and crystals rounding out the other twenty percent. All was well for a few years until disaster struck in 1993. A big chain bookshop opened down the street from me, complete with the parking and discounts which I could not offer. They were large enough to carry all the metaphysical titles I stocked as well as the mainstream books. My business dropped by sixty percent. On top of that, I developed hyperthyroidism from stress and poor diet. I was forced to close my Temple until I felt better and could find a way to salvage my businesses. I leased out the buildings and took some needed rest. During that time I started to connect strongly with the Angel Kingdom. I would ask a question and receive very clear guidance telepathically from my angels. For a brief time I owned an Angel Shop in the Sacramento area. Meanwhile after a year and a half, the people who had leased my property had closed their business. My health had returned and I knew it was time to open my store again. I renamed the shop *Angel Light Books & Gifts* in honor of all the help the Angelic Kingdom had offered me. Instead of featuring mostly books which I had done previously, I expanded my inventory to also include unique spiritual gifts, items that were not available in a chain bookstore. I needed to make the shop inviting enough that customers would not mind having to find street parking and walking some distance to my shop. I placed an angel fountain with fresh flowers encircling the perimeter by the front door.

Scented candles and incense permeated the shop as you entered. Ambient music soothed the soul into a relaxing state. Every angel item imaginable from statuaries, music boxes, lamps, picture frames and candleholder graced glass shelvings. Enchanting fairy figurines perched on nooks and niches. In the Eastern Philosophy Section, I displayed a wealth of feng shui crystals, mirrors, bells and chimes. Statues of Buddha, Quan Yin, Krishna and Shiva highlighted altar tables. I created a secret garden behind the shop and sold a myriad of garden accessories such as fountains, windchimes, birdfeeders, plaques and outdoor statuaries. The result of the makeover was astounding. Customers came from all over the Peninsula for our tranquil ambiance and wondrous assortment of specialty items. My business gradually surpassed my original store. The experience taught me to never give up on my dreams; to expect ups and downs in my career, for that is part of the cycle of life. Obstacles challenge me to build my strength, and impel me to expand my potential and reach new heights.

"A certain amount of opposition is a great help to a person. Kites rise against, not with the wind."

—John Neal

"We see the world not as it is but as we are."

—Anonymous

One of the saddest movies I have ever seen is *You've Got Mail* with Meg Ryan and Tom Hanks. All my friends saw it as a lighthearted romance film. Meanwhile, I went through a whole box of Kleenex crying my eyes out when Meg Ryan's character had to give up her beloved children's bookshop because she couldn't compete with the big chain bookstore that opened down the street. When I related to my friends what a tear-jerker that movie was, they would reply, "What? Are we talking about the same movie?" Apparently having to give up your cherished independent bookshop because of a big corporation did not resonate with them the same way it did me!

Our outer reality is a reflection of what's within. When certain situations push our buttons, we cannot fault the person pushing the button. We need to look at our own core issues if we want to have true healing.

"Life is a mirror and will reflect back
to the thinker what he thinks into it."

—Ernest Holmes

*"If there is harmony in the house, there is order in the nation.
If there is order in the nation, there will be peace in the world."*

—Chinese Proverb

Competition is not a bad thing. It keeps you on your toes and forces you to do a more impeccable job. My store has improved vastly since the opening of a major chain bookstore down the street. It is important not to see another business as competition, nor another country as the enemy. If we can see that we are all one and interconnected to each other as God's family, there will be harmony in our hearts and peace in the world.

In my younger days, I admired the saying from Sun Tsu that translates to, "To win one hundred victories in one hundred battles is not the highest skill. To subdue the enemy without fighting is the highest skill." As I got more evolved, I thought, "Enemy? What enemy? There is no enemy except in our mind's eye."

*"Peace is not the absence of conflict, but the
presence of God no matter what the conflict."*

—Anonymous

*"He who has learned to pray has learned
the greatest secret for a holy and happy life."*

—William Law

A month before my Angel Shop was to open, I was setting up the inventory. On that particular day I was absolutely starving, but because I was expecting a delivery I couldn't leave the store. I knew that God worked miracles, so I began to pray, "God, I am so hungry. Please manifest for me food to appear before me so I can have something to eat. Thank You so much for answered prayers." I trusted that God heard my prayer and was fulfilling my request. I started to unpack the angel items from the day before. When I opened the box, I found bags and bags of popcorn wrapped in plastic bags. In the box was a note that read, "We decided to pack your parcel with edible popcorn today instead of styrofoam peanuts. Enjoy!" It was like manna from Heaven. I have never tasted popcorn so good before, perhaps because it was a gift from God. That was the only time I ever received popcorn from that company, or any other company, again.

*"God eagerly awaits the chance to bless the person
whose heart is turned towards Him."*

—Anonymous

*"Behold the turtle. He makes progress
only when he sticks his neck out."*

—James Bryant Conant

I once had a regular customer who had a dream of opening his own healing center. He had all the details planned out in his mind, but he would not do anything tangible to make it happen. He was always waiting for the perfect timing, right contacts and ideal situations before he would proceed. I told him, "Sometimes you need to take the plunge and things will unfold once you get started." As Will Rogers said, "Even if you are on the right track, you'll get run over if you just sit there." Meanwhile he would pass up on many wonderful opportunities to fulfill his dream.

When I first started my business I knew nothing about opening up a bookstore. In the pre-internet days, it took much more time and effort to find companies that sold books, music, incense, candles, crystals, meditation supplies and store fixtures. Knowing what titles and subjects to stock was a hit-and-miss situation. After a few years in business, companies began to find *me* and I developed a better selection of merchandise. With experience, I started to know what categories my customers were interested in. It takes trial and error, but it was a matter of getting my feet wet and just doing it. If I waited until I knew everything, I would never have gotten started. It is in *taking the action first* that things began to unfold for me.

*"Be not afraid of growing slowly,
be afraid only of standing still."*

—Chinese Proverb

*"The royal road to success would have more travelers
if so many weren't lost attempting to find short cuts."*

—H. C. Calvin

A massage therapist came to my shop one day to post her business card on my bulletin board. She announced, "I desperately need money. I hope I can get some clients from this." She handed me her business cards which were warped and dirty. The phone number and address were crossed out and she had handwritten the correct number and location on it. Meanwhile, I have more than fifty cards posted on my bulletin board—if you want to get noticed you have to do better than that! Another massage therapist came in with a beautifully designed business card and flyer. On the flyer was a pouch where she had inserted stacks of certificates for $20 off the first visit. Who do you think will get the clients?

*"Striving for success without hard work is like
trying to harvest where you haven't planted."*

—David Bly

"Better to do something and fail,
than to do nothing and succeed."

—Robert Schuller

When my Virgo friend (who shall remain nameless) found out I was going to produce my own line of aromatherapy products for the store, he groaned, "Here you go again, more money down the drain. I can see another flop. Remember the time you opened for brunch and invested all the money printing menus and buying supplies, only to find out starting early wasn't your thing?" I notice my Virgo friend is very good at reminding me of my failures but never my triumphs. I keep him around because he works for me and, quite frankly, I couldn't manage the place without him. As a Virgo he is efficient and organized and does the work of three people. But as a Virgo he is also critical, skeptical and judgmental. If you want a cheerleader to rally you on, he is not the one to have. One of the laws of manifesting is to not share your ideas with non-supportive people. But my resolve was strong enough that nothing was going to deter me. As it turned out, my line of hand-blended aromatherapy products continues to be one of the best-selling items in the shop.

"He that is overcautious will accomplish little."

—JCF von Schiller

"If a man is called to be a street sweeper, he should sweep streets
as Michelangelo painted, or Beethoven composed music, or
Shakespeare wrote poetry. He should sweep streets so well
that all the hosts of Heaven and Earth will pause to say,
here lived a great street sweeper who did his job well."

—Martin Luther King Jr.

I see a pattern in many of my metaphysical acquaintances who are unfulfilled in their jobs because they want to do something spiritual with their lives. It is not that they have any specific dream that they want to pursue, or that they are unhappy at work, they just want to be making more of a difference in people's lives. Spirituality is something you *are*, not what you *do*. You could be making a difference in people's lives no matter what occupation you had. If you are working in an office where you are the one constantly bringing peace and harmony to the staff, perhaps *that* is where you are needed. A woman I know was working for the city where she helped people find affordable housing. Her compassionate ways always put her clients at ease. Yet she would lament, "I wish I could quit my mainstream job and do something spiritual with my life." You can be collecting money in a toll booth and make a difference with your loving presence, kind words or genuine smile.

"You can do no great things,
only small things with great love."

—Mother Theresa

"Some people grumble because the roses have thorns instead of being grateful that the thorns have roses."

—Anonymous

A woman who used to frequent my shop would always share with me her woes and problems. No matter what positive feedback I gave her, she would be back to square-one with her negativity. Little did she know that her negative thoughts were attracting more negativity to her. What a difference her life would be if she would magnify her blessings the way she did her problems.

In the 15 years I owned my businesses, there were many years that the only way I could pay my bills was by working seven days a week, ten hours a day. Since I loved what I did, I didn't really consider it work, but it would have been nice to have more financial flow. In my meditation I would ask my angels why I wasn't more successful. The soft whisper I received was *"Do not measure success by how many meals are served, or how much dollars are spent, but how much light you are adding to consciousness."* Indeed, there were many days that people would come to my shop not to buy anything, but to soak up the peaceful ambiance. People in recovery from alcoholism would tell me when they have an urge to drink, coming to my shop would help them reconnect with their Higher Power. It reminds me how truly blessed I am that I can make a difference in another's life. I needed to stop focusing on what I didn't have and be thankful for all the blessings I did have.

"The optimist sees the doughnut, the pessimist the hole."

—Mc Landburgh Wilson

*"Pure and simple, any person who
is enjoying life is a success."*

—William Feather

I am not computer literate. All my inventory are recorded in a spiral note-book. When I sell a book or wish to add a new title, I jot it down and place my order by phone. It's worked for me for 15 years. And is that such a bad thing? How healthy is it to sit in front of a computer monitor absorbing all that electro-magnetic frequency? I wonder how many young people who are diagnosed as hyperactive today just need to get outside more? They stay cooped up in a classroom all day long and then sit in front of a computer for hours on end. No wonder they are restless and inattentive! What happened to the olden days when Timmy would go out in nature with Lassie, absorbing fresh air and getting some exercise? We'd never heard of attention-deficit disorder nor prescribing drugs to kids back then.

Being a business owner, everybody tells me how important it is to have e-mail, so I gave it a try. For me it was a hassle to unplug my phone line and connect my computer only to receive junk mail from heaven-knows-who. It was constantly jam crammed with unwanted mail that I would need to spend the day deleting, until I finally just gave up. I'm a Cancer with my moon in Libra. I prefer to do things the old-fashioned way. All my correspondence have always been hand-written on pretty stationery with matching envelopes to boot! I will include my e-mail address in this book in case, by some miracle, I have mastered the computer. But if you e-mail me and don't hear from me for awhile, I may be out in my garden absorbing the scent of roses while writing my response by hand.

"What was paradise but a garden."

—William Cole

Astrology

"He who knows others is wise.
He who knows himself is enlightenment."

—Tao Te Ching

When we were born, we all came with a manual—our astrological chart. Our astrological chart is a snapshot of the planets' positions in the sky at the precise moment of our birth. Like a snowflake, there are no two alike—each is unique and unrepeatable. I find most people don't take advantage of the wealth of information available in their charts. They go through years of trying to find their right vocation when one's horoscope can reveal one's strengths, talents and optimal career choices. In relationships your horoscope can reveal to you what type of partners you are attracted to, your ideal mate and how you tend to relate to others. If you have the birthchart of the person you are with, you can cast a compatibility chart and discover more about your partner and what gifts and challenges the relationship offers. By truly understanding ourselves and others we can save years of contention and conflict. We learn to accept others for who they are and not try to change them. All the signs are endowed with wonderful qualities and the world would not be complete without everyone's contributions.

The transits in your chart tell you how the planets' current positions are affecting your horoscope. Timing is everything. When we ride the current, things flow better and doors open magically. As I am writing this book, Jupiter—the planet of favorable opportunity, expansion and growth—is transiting my 9th house, the house of wisdom, philosophy and publication. In my natal chart I have Pluto in my 9th house which is being activated by Jupiter. By next year, Jupiter will be entering my 10th house adding opportunity, expansion and growth to my house of career and success. In my birthchart I have four planets in my house of career that will be affected by this transit. The next two years will be a favorable time to get my book published and bring more recognition to my career. If I don't take advantage of the opportunity *now* I will have to wait another *12 years* for the next cycle!

To get started, you need a copy of your astrological chart. You can get your chart cast in minutes with a computer. I'm not a big fan of computerized interpretation because you are missing the human factor of synthesis, intuition and experience. Even if you have a reading with a reputable astrologer, you might want to continue to learn more on your own. There are many wonderful books that can help you gain more insights about your chart.

We never finish learning about ourselves and others because we evolve, we meet new people and the changing cycle of the planets affect our horoscope. Our chart is a gift from God to give us more self-awareness, help us to reach our highest potential, and guide us along life's path.

Feng Shui

Feng Shui literally means *wind and water* and refers to the tangible and intangible forces of nature. Practiced in China for more than 3000 years, it is the science and art of arranging one's surroundings to bring the most auspicious energy and flow. Feng shui combines the balance of *yin* and *yang*, the harmonious blend of the five elements—wood, fire, earth, metal and water—the flow of *chi* and the ancient wisdom of the *bagua*. The study of feng shui is intricate and vast, with volumes of books devoted to the subject. There are basic techniques one can practice without being proficient in feng shui.

One of the most effective feng shui treatments is to clear your clutter. Clutter represents stuck energy. Wherever you see clutter in relationship to the *bagua* is where you will experience obstacles. For instance, if the wealth area of your home is cluttered, you would experience blocked energy concerning money. Clutter stagnates and constricts the beneficial *chi* from spreading easily throughout the house. Look around your home and see where you have piles of junk, old papers and clothes that serve no purpose in your life. Observe where you have things you no longer love, use or need. Release them and make room for better things to come into your life. All things in the universe are endowed with a life force energy called *chi*. If you love something, it is alive with *vibrant chi*. Conversely, if you hate something, it is filled with *depleting chi*—your energy level and that of your home drops just by having it in your space. When you fill your home with things that are meaningful and sacred to you, your life becomes meaningful and sacred.

The *bagua* represents the eight areas of one's life which includes career, knowledge, family, wealth, fame, relationships, children and helpful people. Suffice it to say, more people ask me about the wealth section than all the other seven combined. The wealth area is located on the far left corner of a room or house, viewing the area from the main entrance.

Here are some basic wealth enhancement tips:

- **Place a healthy green plant** in your wealth section to signify that your money is growing and flourishing.

- **Display a fountain** in your wealth area to represent money flowing in your life. In China, water is associated with money so be sure to refill the water as it evaporates and that your pump works to ensure a continuous flow.

- **For people who have a bathroom in the wealth section**, money has a tendency to "go down the drain," or it can have the effect of money being flushed down the toilet. Be sure to keep the toilet lid down and the door to your bathroom closed. Since the wealth section is ruled by the element wood, you can hang wallpaper of plants or flowers in your bathroom to symbolize money growing, mitigating the effect of the drains.

- **If you have a window in your wealth area**, money tends to "go out the window" as soon as it comes in. Hang a round, faceted crystal ball by the window. When the sunlight hits the crystal it forms a beautiful rainbow that circulates the energy back into the room.

It is important that you *set your intent* when you do your feng shui treatments. One time I had suggested a client hang a faceted crystal ball in the wealth section of her business because she had a floor-to-ceiling window there. I told her to focus her intent on creating prosperity when she hung the crystal and say a positive affirmation such as: "I am prosperous," "Money flows into my business," or "I magnetize an abundance of clients and money." She noticed a tremendous improvement in her business after doing the treatment. A year later she called to convey that someone had taken her crystal, so she was sending her sister to pick up another one. After a few weeks she came back to the shop to say that the second crystal did not work and asked if I had changed brands of crystals. I answered no, but I intuitively sensed that the second crystal was not hung with the same intent as the first. When I shared that with her, she immediately gasped, "You're right! My sister hung that second crystal. Not only does she not believe in feng shui, she is the the most negative person!" Every time sunlight hit the second crystal, thoughts of lack and negativity infused the space.

Another customer had major clutter in her wealth area. I told her she needed to clear out the clutter in order for money to flow into her life. She resisted the advice and pleaded, "I heard purple is the color for the money section. Can't I just put a purple amethyst crystal from the shop there instead?" Even though that would have resulted in a huge purchase for the store, I could not suggest that she do that. Crystals, as well as mirrors, augment energy and all it would have done was amplify the chaos and clutter in her wealth section. So remember to always clear your clutter prior to adding crystals or mirrors to your environment.

If your wealth section is missing—meaning if the rest of your house extends further back and your wealth area is indented—it represents lack of money. To counteract the effect, hang a mirror there to visually extend the space deeper. I once had a client with that problem, but the missing wealth section had a window there which made it inappropriate to hang a mirror. He lived on the second floor and outside the window was the roof to the back of the house. I suggested he hang a colorful fish windsock on the pole outside where the roof was. The flapping movement of the wind-sock would call in chi to his money section, and the image of a fish is synonymous with abundance in China. When I saw him the next day he was amazed how fast the feng shui treatment had worked. Shortly after he hung the windsock he received a call from someone who wanted to pur-chase $1500 worth of his sculptures which had sat idle for many months. Feng Shui always works. It is an invaluable tool that can bring harmony, flow and fortunate blessings into any area of your life.

Aromatherapy

I was first exposed to aromatherapy as a small child. Whenever I had ailments of any kind my mother would bring out that one bottle of Chinese medicine called *White Flower Oil*. This bottle contained a variety of essential aromatherapy oils, two of the most prominent being eucalyptus and lavender. *Eucalyptus Oil* is used for respiratory problems, congestion, colds, flu, fever, muscular aches, arthritic pain, as well as anything requiring antiseptic, antibiotic or antiviral properties. *Lavender Oil* is used for insect bites, stings, poison ivy, burns, cold sores, asthma, bronchitis, headaches and insomnia. It was basically an all-purpose remedy in one bottle. In traditional Chinese medicine, people did not have a whole pharmacy in their medicine cabinet like Westerners do. For thousands of years they have relied solely on natural herbs and essential oils for healing. One bottle of White Flower Oil even today costs less than five dollars. It works wonderfully well and has no drugs or side effects. Here is one solution to the rising cost of health care!

Besides medicinal uses, aromatherapy has wonderful therapeutic benefits on the emotional and mental body:

- *Lemon Oil* uplifts the soul and brings cheer in times of depression.

- *Chamomile* promotes a sense of inner peace and calmness.

- *Sandalwood* quiets the mind and deepens one's meditations.

- *Rosemary* enhances mental clarity, concentration and memory.

- *Lavender* clears negativity from one's aura and environment.

- *Rose Oil* soothes the heart and invokes a sense of beauty and harmony.

In 1999, I decided to create my own blend of aromatherapy products for my shop. For months I gathered rose petals and geranium florets from my enchanted garden to dry. I mixed them with lavender, jasmine, rosemary and essential oils to create my *Love Blossoms Potpourri*. To make my *Angel Blessings Potpourri*, I blended angelica, sandalwood, frankincense, marigold and chamomile, and sold them in apothecary jars with cork lids. The irresistible scent of a summer garden permeated the shop even during the dormant season of winter. One of my best-selling items turned out to be my *Purification Aroma Mist*. For a quick pick-me-up you can spray it on yourself to clear your aura or use it in your environment to purify your space. Our ten blends of massage oils continue to be sought after by massage therapists and retail customers alike.

As I work with essential oils, I find myself attuning to the wondrous realm of plants, flowers and nature spirits. They are truly God's gift to humankind to bless us with their alluring beauty, delightful scent and marvelous healing properties.

Flower Remedies

One of my favorite healing products—that I think more people should know about—are flower remedies. Discovered in the 1930s by Dr. Edward Bach, flower remedies are liquid plant extracts prescribed to promote harmony between one's emotional and mental state. Taken internally by ingesting four drops, four times daily for 30 days (longer or shorter duration can be used depending on the condition) will bring about phenomenal changes. Because flower remedies are a form of vibrational medicine, they can never cause harm and can be safely administered to adults, children, pets, and even plants.

The two flower remedies that have helped me immensely are *Mimulus* and *Larch*. Being extremely shy and self-conscious growing up, expressing myself was always a challenge. If I could leave my mark on the world—and be invisible at the same time—I would do it! But my destiny was to be out in public sharing my ideas and expressing my creativity. Mimulus has helped me develop a stronger constitution and overcome my fear of self-expression. Because mimulus helps with building courage, it is also an ideal remedy for fear issues in general: fear of heights, fear of public speaking, fear of snakes, fear of flying, fear of going to the dentist…the list can go on indefinitely. If you are having an extreme panic attack, take the *rescue remedy* (also called *five flower remedy*), but if you are looking to gradually overcome a phobia, mimulus is the one to use. And quite frankly, who doesn't have fears? If more people knew about these remarkable remedies, they would be flocking to my store!

The other remedy that has helped me personally is larch. Larch is recommended for people who lack self-confidence and have an inferiority complex. It is instrumental for people who are starting a new job or business and are plagued with self-doubt and fear of failure. Larch can also be prescribed for children who perhaps do not feel as popular or as smart as their classmates and want to improve their low self-esteem. Other popular remedies I have suggested to people include:

- ***Aspen*** is recommended for people who are prone to needless worry, nervousness and paranoia. These are the people who tend to dwell on negativity and seem to have a foreboding dread without probable cause. You can also administer aspen to your pets. If you have a cat that is skittish, easily scared and jumps at the slightest provocation, a few drops of aspen in their food will bring greater strength, courage and trust.
- ***Elm*** is encouraged for people who are overwhelmed by responsibility. They tend to take on too much and have a hard time asking for help. Taking elm releases the stress by giving the individual a greater level of confidence to handle the task, and the ability to ask for assistance where needed.
- ***Holly*** is prescribed for individuals dealing with intense emotions like hatred, jealousy and revenge. It softens the negative emotions by bringing a greater level of tolerance and love.
- ***Mustard or Gorse*** works for depression, depending on the severity of the condition. For people who are feeling blue and going through a down cycle, mustard can help uplift one's spirit. If the individual is deeply depressed, suffering from extreme despair and have a feeling of complete hopelessness, gorse would be a source of relief.
- ***Walnut*** is an excellent remedy for individuals who are going through a change or transition. If you are moving to a new home, going through a job transition, or a woman going through "the change," taking walnut will be most beneficial. You can even add a few drops of walnut to soil if you are repotting a plant or transplanting it to another location.
- ***Willow*** is advised for people who are resentful and bitter regarding a person or situation. They tend to dwell in the past and have a hard time forgiving and letting go. Taking willow helps release blame so one can move forward in life.

There are 38 different remedies to assist in a myriad of conditions. Learn more about the wonderful world of flower remedies and see if there are some that could enhance your life.

Crystals and Stones

The mineral kingdom is part of Earth's consciousness along with the plant, animal and human kingdoms. Just as there are nature spirits that work with the plant kingdom, animal spirits that guard over animals, and the angelic realm that watches over humans, the mineral kingdom has earth devas that reside with them. Try gazing at your quartz crystal and see if you can detect the image of a deva among the mists and veils. Ask if it has a message for you. Clairvoyants who are very sensitive to energy can hold a crystal and impart much wisdom from the mineral kingdom. When we learn to attune to all of God's creations we develop a oneness and reverence for all life.

Clear Quartz

Clear quartz, sometimes described as frozen light, offers a bridge between the physical realm and spiritual realm. Used in silicon chips, quartz makes modern technology possible; as a metaphysical tool it makes the interdimensional realm attainable.

Quartz is invaluable in computers and tape recorders because of its ability to store energy. You can take quartz crystal and program it by holding it and reciting positive affirmations to it. Whenever you come in contact with the crystal, you would absorb the favorable message embedded in the crystal. Quartz is used in speakers and microphones because of its capacity to amplify energy. You can hold a quartz crystal while you meditate, pray or visualize, and your session will be augmented with more power and intensity. Quartz is essential to radios because of its potential to transmit energy waves. You can use quartz crystal as a healing wand and direct the laser beam of light to your objective.

Crystals and stones absorb energy so it is important to clear them upon purchase, or if one has been in a negative space while using them. One technique to clear the crystals is to soak them in a large bowl of water with a tablespoon of sea salt for a few hours and envision the salt absorbing all impurities. Another method is to hold the crystal under running luke-warm water for about 30 seconds and visualize all negativity washing down the drain. An alternate approach is to bury the crystal in the earth overnight or longer and imagine the soil soaking up all the impurities. Rinse afterwards with clear water. If you have a large piece or if you have many crystals and stones to clear at once, you can burn a smudge stick over them and allow the smoke to purify them of any negativity. Clear quartz, because it is colorless, can embody the properties of all the stones making it one of the most versatile minerals.

☙

Your Astrological Stone

Each astrological sign has a special stone assigned to it to enhance the bearer's life. Different from your birthstone, which is based on the month you are born, your astrological stone matches your personality with your most compatible stone. If you consult different books, your astrological stone may vary since they are based on the author's interpretation. To introduce customers to gemstones, at one time I gave them an astrological stone if it was the month of their birthday. I included information in my newsletter of the meaning of the stones. Here is a synopsis of what I wrote:

♈ *Aries*
Planetary Ruler: **Mars** • Color: **Red** • Stone: **Red Jasper**

Aries, being the first sign of the zodiac, are initiative, impulsive and impatient. The Warrior of the Zodiac, they are imbued with courage and valor. *Red Jasper* is the stone for strength, courage and vitality. It gives one the stamina and fortitude to handle life's many challenges.

♉ *Taurus*
Planetary Ruler: **Venus** • Color: **Green** • Stone: **Green Aventurine**

Taureans are stable and calm people who love nature and are very down to earth. Patient and dependable, they are also known to be stubborn. *Green aventurine* calms and stabilizes the emotions. Like the color of a healthy plant, its soothing green is harmonizing and comforting.

♊ *Gemini*
Planetary Ruler: **Mercury** • Color: **Sky Blue** • Stone: **Blue Lace Agate**

Geminis, being an air sign, are the Communicators of the Zodiac. They are versatile and changeable, and are famous for their inquisitive minds. *Blue Lace Agate* is the stone for enhancing clarity of mind and creative self-expression. Its tranquil blue color provides a calming effect for Gemini's restless nature.

♋ *Cancer*
Planetary Ruler: **The Moon** • Color: **Silvery Blue** • Stone: **Moonstone**

Cancers are known as the Mother of the Zodiac because of their nurturing and caring nature. Highly intuitive and sensitive they are guided by their emotions. *Moonstone* with its milky sheen is ruled by lunar influences. It can be used to alleviate feminine conditions such as fertility, pregnancy,

PMS and menopause. When utilized by men, it stimulates the right side of the brain encouraging non-linear thinking and emotional balance.

♌ *Leo*
Planetary Ruler: **The Sun** • Color: **Golden Yellow** • Stone: **Citrine**

Leos are known to be proud and confident. Ruled by the Sun, they are sunny, warm-hearted people who love to take center stage. Magnanimous and generous by nature, they need to be appreciated. The golden color of *Citrine* exudes warmth, cheerfulness and joy. It enhances one's self-esteem and personal power.

♍ *Virgo*
Planetary Ruler: **Mercury** • Color: **Brown** • Stone: **Botswana Agate**

Virgos, being an earth sign, are practical, efficient and organized people. Perfectionistic and meticulous, they have a good eye for details. The mercury rulership provides for them their analytical and logical minds. *Botswana Agate*, with its brown and white band, is grounding for the body and stabilizing for the mind. It helps one integrate the intellectual realm into the physical plane.

♎ *Libra*
Planetary Ruler: **Venus** • Color: **Pink** • Stone: **Rose Quartz**

Libras are refined people who admire beauty and art. They are known to be the Peacemaker of the Zodiac. Because partnership rules their sign, relationships play a key role in their lives. *Rose Quartz*, also known as the love stone, enhances one's capacity to give love and to receive love. Wearing this soft pink stone adds the qualities of beauty, gentleness and peace to one's aura.

♏ *Scorpio*

Planetary Ruler: **Pluto** • Color: **Black** & **Maroon Red** • Stone: **Obsidian**

Scorpios rule power, transformation, death, rebirth and sex. Noted for their intensity and magnetism, they are often drawn to the mysterious world of the occult. *Obsidian* absorbs negativity and transforms it to a higher vibration. Because it holds energy, it is important to cleanse often. The black color of obsidian is both grounding and helpful in dealing with life's crises.

♐ *Sagittarius*

Planetary Ruler: **Jupiter** • Color: **Deep Blue** • Stone: **Sodalite**

Sagittarians are the Truthseekers of the Zodiac. Freedom loving and adventurous, they seek to broaden their horizon through travel. They are known to be philosophical and wise as well as optimistic and jovial. *Sodalite* opens one's clairvoyant ability by removing the veil of illusion and allowing one to see truth. Its dark blue color deepens one's capacity for wisdom and knowledge.

♑ *Capricorn*

Planetary Ruler: **Saturn** • Color: **Gray** • Stone: **Hematite**

Capricorns are ambitious people. They are the goats climbing the mountain. Persevering and determined, they are willing to take one step at a time until they reach the pinnacle of success. *Hematite*, being one of the heaviest stones, is extremely grounding and keeps one focused on one's path. Its metallic gray color matches the somber and serious tone of Capricorn.

♒ *Aquarius*

Planetary Ruler: **Uranus** • Color: **Electric Blue** • Stone: **Aquamarine**

Aquarians are the Humanitarian of the Zodiac. They are friendly yet emotionally detached. Independent and unpredictable, they like to march to the beat of their own drummer. Aquarians are eccentric people known for their brilliant and innovative minds. *Aquamarine*, with its soft blue color, is soothing for the nerves and calming for the mind. It brings clarity to one's creative ideas and the ability to express them.

♓ *Pisces*

Planetary Ruler: **Neptune** • Color: **Purple** • Stone: **Amethyst**

Pisces is the sign for spirituality, mysticism and psychic ability. The Visionary of the Zodiac, they are also the artists, poets and dreamers. *Amethyst* is an excellent stone to deepen one's meditation and enhance one's psychic abilities. Its iridescent purple color opens up the higher channels and connects one to the spiritual realms.

☙

    I once wore a rose quartz heart pendant while I was going through a painful separation. I was so engrossed in my sorrow that I didn't even think of cleansing it. The poor rose quartz absorbed all my sadness until it eventually cracked and broke. I gave it a burial and thanked it for sacrificing itself to provide a healing for me.

    When customers ask me about the different meanings of the stones, I like to have them choose one that they are drawn to among the hundreds on my counter. Invariably they will choose a stone that their soul most needs without prior knowledge of its significance. One woman chose a blue lace agate. I told her that the stone was to help one communicate their deepest truth. She was amazed for she had just come from her marriage counselor who told her she needed to speak her truth more with her husband.

Another time, a set of twin sisters came to my shop. One of the sisters went to the restroom while her twin chose a stone and asked me what it meant. She had picked a red jasper. I informed her that red jasper was the stone for courage and fearlessness. She said that was exactly what she needed because she was leaving an abusive husband and required the strength to move on. When her sister returned, we asked her to choose a stone. Without knowing what her sister picked, she chose the red jasper also. It turned out that both twins were going through the same thing—leaving an abusive relationship!

Another woman wanted to know what stone she should buy. I said, "Choose what you are drawn to." She picked a brown tiger eye. I told her that tiger eye, being the color of the earth, was good for stability and groundedness. She replied that it was just what she needed because she was a flight attendant and felt extremely ungrounded from all the extra traveling and flying she had been doing lately. She said she was exhausted and needed to connect with the earth again.

An alternate method, besides choosing a stone by the color you are drawn to, is to ask yourself what color is your *least* favorite. Oftentimes that is the color you most need because it is the one you are deficient in.

One time a man was choosing stones he was drawn to so I could interpret their meanings for him. Every stone he chose was either black, brown or gray. I inquired what sign he was and he told me he was a Capricorn. The serious, nose-to-the-grindstone Capricorn was drawn to earth-toned stones that corresponded to groundedness, stability and hard work. I asked him what color he absolutely hated and without hesitation he replied "yellow." I said, "Buy a yellow stone, for that is what your soul most needs. Yellow is the color of joy, cheerfulness and light-heartedness." He laughed when I said that and revealed that he was often annoyed by easy-going, fun-loving people because it was the side of himself he most denied.

To create balance in your life, have a collection of stones representing all the spectrums of the rainbow. Use your intuition and choose a stone you are drawn to on that day and carry it with you. Or close your eyes and have your Higher Self choose what you most need from amongst your collection.

ॐ

Crystal Healing

The colors of the crystals correspond to the seven "Chakra," from the Sanskrit word meaning wheel. The spinning wheels of light are actually vortices of energy that flow through our physical bodies. Each Chakra is associated with a part of the body and a certain color or colors.

To do crystal healing, one method is to lie down and place the stone(s) in the areas that relate to the Chakra. For instance, if one is experiencing fear, they would have a weakened 2nd Chakra, located in the lower abdominal area. The lower abdomen is where one would experience "butterflies" in their stomach, anxiety and nervousness. Lie down and place a carnelian stone there and visualize the color orange infusing your lower abdomen with strength and confidence. Because the color orange is made by blending red and yellow, you might want to put corresponding stones in your 1st and 3rd Chakras since they would have a tendency to be depleted as well.

When a Chakra is deficient, the color is weak and the spinning of the vortex faint. An imbalance, where the Chakra is excessive, shows up as a mass of murky, muddled shade rather than a bright and vibrant color. To have a prominent Chakra is not necessarily unhealthy as long as the color is radiant and clear.

Here is a list of the basic meanings of the Chakras, colors and stones:

Chakra: *1st Chakra*, also known as the root Chakra, located at the base of the spine.

Colors: Black, Brown and Gray

Function: Matters relating to the material world, groundedness, survival, security

Deficient: Lower back pain, worry over money, ungroundedness, inability to survive in the material world

Excessive: Materialistic, greed, workaholic

Stones: Obsidian, onyx, black tourmaline, apache tears, jet, smokey quartz, hematite, tiger iron, boji stones, petrified wood, botswana agate

---

Chakra: *1st Chakra* located at the base of the spine.

Color: Red

Function: Life force energy, vitality, physical stamina, courage, will power, passion, enthusiasm

Deficient: Chronic fatigue syndrome, lack of energy, afraid to stand up for oneself, weakness

Excessive: Anger, domination, agressiveness

Stones: Red jasper, garnet, ruby, red tiger eye, red goldstone, bloodstone for both 1st and 4th Chakras

---

Chakra: *2nd Chakra* located at the lower abdomen area, near pelvis.

Color: Orange

Function: Strength, confidence, sociability, gut feelings, emotion, sexual desire, intimacy, pleasure

Deficient: Fear, timidity, sexual repression

Excessive: Arrogance, indulgence, preoccupation with sex

Stones: Carnelian, coral, peach aventurine, orange calcite, golden tiger eye, moonstone, leopard skin jasper, zincite

Chakra: *3rd Chakra* located at the solar plexus, center between the navel and chest area.

Color: Yellow

Function: Mental clarity, warm and sunny disposition, joy, cheerfulness, self-esteem, personal power

Deficient: Mental confusion, despondency, depression, low self-esteem

Excessive: Overly cerebral, self-centered, autocratic

Stones: Citrine, honey calcite, amber, yellow topaz, yellow sapphire, rutilated quartz, sunstone

Chakra: *4th Chakra* located at the heart center.

Color: Green

Function: Harmony, balance, health, peace, forgiveness, compassion

Deficient: Resentment, unforgiveness, emotional imbalance

Excessive: Bleeding heart, martyr, sacrificing

Stones: Aventurine, emerald, green jade, green tourmaline, peridot, malachite, moldavite, dioptase, green fluorite, moss agate, chrysoprase, apophyllite, unikite, bloodstone

Chakra: *4th Chakra* located at the heart center.

Color: Pink

Function: Love, unconditional love, giving and receiving love, beauty, kindness, gentleness, softness

Deficient: Feeling unlovable, withholding love, hardheartedness

Excessive: Passive, submissive, inability to say no

Stones:	Rose quartz, pink tourmaline, kunzite, rhodochrosite, rhodonite, morganite

Chakra:	***5th Chakra*** located at the throat center.
Color:	Light blue
Function:	Communication, truth, creative expression, clairaudient ability, calmness, tranquility, serenity
Deficient:	Sore throat, not expressing oneself, creatively blocked, stress
Excessive:	Verbose, argumentative, self-righteous
Stones:	Aquamarine, blue lace agate, blue quartz, blue calcite, blue topaz, turquoise, chrysocolla, angelite, kyanite, amazonite, celestite, larimar

Chakra:	***6th Chakra*** located at the third eye between the eye brows.
Colors:	Deep blue, indigo
Function:	Clairvoyant ability, psychic power, insight, intuition, imagination, visualization, wisdom, knowledge
Deficient:	Denying intuition, inability to imagine or visualize, not seeing clearly, lacking wisdom
Excessive:	Obsessed with the occult and supernatural, hallucinating, dogmatic
Stones:	Lapis, sodalite, azurite, apatite, sapphire, danburite, dumortierite, iolite

Chakra:	***7th Chakra*** located at the crown of head.
Colors:	Purple, violet
Function:	Spirituality, inspiration, meditation, Higher Consciousness, connection with the Divine, oneness with all life

Deficient: Not connecting with a Higher Power, lack of inspiration, distrust, separation

Excessive: Spacey, delusional, out of touch with reality

Stones: Amethyst, sugilite, purple fluorite, purple jade, charoite, lepidolite, tanzanite

---

Chakra: ***All Chakras***

Colors: White or Clear

Function: White light, protection, purification, properties of all colors

Stones: Clear quartz, selenite, diamond, white calcite, white howlite

Cherish God's Gift to Humankind

Step into the magical world of the Mineral Kingdom and Earth Devas.
Dare to choose a stone and see what insightful message it has for you.

The Animal Kingdom

Since ancient times, people all around the world have revered animals for their power and wisdom. The Druids from Scandinavia believed that if certain animals showed up in your life, physically or in dreams, they had a message for you. For instance:

- *Bear* was revered for their strength and power. Because the bear is associated with the guiding Pole Star of the Great Bear, it indicates following one's intuition for guidance. Encountering bear energy reminds us that one does not have true power unless one connects with their inner source.

- *Butterfly* denotes freedom, transformation and rebirth. Going from larvae to caterpillar to butterfly, they signify eternity and awaken us to the concept that there is no death, only change.

- *Cats* often served as familiars for witches because of their ability to exist in the physical and spiritual realm simultaneously. They were often affiliated with goddess energy and feminine power.

- *Fox* represented using wit and slyness to outsmart one's opponent. The fox also has the gift of adaptability and the skill to become invisible by camouflaging themselves from their enemy.

- *Raven* with its deep black color personifies magic, mystery and the occult. Being scavengers who feed off the corpses of the dead, the ravens were suggestive of bad luck and omens of death. In truth, the raven has the gift of clairvoyance and the capacity for healing.

- *Squirrels* teach us to store our resources for future use. They caution us that in life there are always peaks and valleys and to be prepared under any circumstances.

The Native Americans maintained that everyone is born with a specific totem animal that protects and guides them throughout their lives. They would also invoke or pray to various animal spirits to call forth their medicine power. For example:

- *Buffalo* symbolize abundance. All parts of the buffalo were used; the flesh for food, the fur for clothing, the hide for shelter and the horns for tools. The Native Americans saw the sacredness of all life and knew to give thanks for God's bounty.

- *Deer* embody innocence, grace and gentleness. They demonstrate that love, softness and compassion can overcome any hard conditions.

- *Eagle* exemplifies inner vision, illumination and connection to Divine Spirit. They are invoked for their ability to soar and reach great heights.

- *Frogs*, being linked with water, represent cleansing, emotional healing and metamorphosis.

- *Turtle* indicates long life, endurance and patience. They prompt us to slow down and go within for reflection before moving forward.

- *Wolves* travel in packs and epitomize loyalty, perseverance and guardianship. They are also the pathfinders and teachers.

The Chinese believed that the Zodiac animal of your birth year has much to teach you. For a complete chart your birthdate would be considered for the rising sign and ruling element. Here are the basic attributes of the twelve astrological animals.

- *Rats* are clever resourceful creatures who know how to hoard up for a rainy day (thus the term "pack rat"). Recognized for being materialistic and a bit of an opportunist, they get by in life through their charm and wit.

ʿᴓᴈ **Ox** has the ability to plod one-step-at-a-time, which makes them solid, reliable and methodical. Hardworking and stubborn, they are noted to be traditional, conservative and family-oriented.

ʿᴓᴈ **Tigers** are powerful and courageous. They have leadership ability and hate to follow orders. As a rebel they dislike authority figures or the status quo.

ʿᴓᴈ **Rabbits** are known for their calm, docile, peaceful demeanor. Artistic and refined, they have a taste for the finer things in life.

ʿᴓᴈ **Dragons**, one of the most illustrious and dynamic signs are capable of succeeding at almost anything. Their confidence and magnetic personality wins them the support of their followers.

ʿᴓᴈ **Snakes** are the deep thinker of the Zodiac. They are mysterious, philosophical and wise. Beautiful and sensuous, the snake can be possessive and have been known to twine their coils around their beloved.

ʿᴓᴈ **Horses** are freedom-loving spirits who do not like to be fenced in. Gregarious and outgoing, they like to kick up their heels and have a good time. Being both self-reliant and independent, they can excel in any field that allows them free rein.

ʿᴓᴈ **Sheep** are easy-going, mild-mannered types who prefer to follow rather than lead. They are sympathetic and compassionate souls who are willing to help those less fortunate than themselves. They, in turn, are always blessed with the three most important things in life—food, clothing and shelter.

ʿᴓᴈ **Monkeys** are bright, quick-witted and innovative people who can solve intricate problems with ease. Cunning and sly, they can excel in any field that requires mental dexterity.

☞ **Roosters** are flamboyant and dashing souls who like to strut proudly in the finest of attire. They are notorious for being frank and direct, and are not afraid to speak their minds. Fastidious and meticulous, they are adept at handling anything that requires organizational skills.

☞ **Dogs** have a deep sense of loyalty and will protect those they love. Honest, trustworthy and with a high sense of morality, they are often seen fighting the injustices of the world.

☞ **Pigs**, being affable, sincere and guileless, will always have friends willing to help them. Innocent and naïve, the pig tends to be lucky in money and destined to live a life of comfort and luxury.

What animals are you drawn to? Have animals comes into your life physically or in your dreams? Discover your totem animal; explore the wisdom of your Chinese astrological sign. There are many splendid books devoted to the animal kingdom. Learn what gifts and wisdom they have to offer you.

Finis

Afterword

One morning while meditating I received a very clear message, "Write your book." I protested, "I don't know anything about writing a book." The gentle whisper replied, "You didn't know anything about building this Temple either, yet you didn't let that stop you." My mind immediately flashed back 15 years earlier when I first embarked on this venture. I had to muster the courage to leave everything that was secure and comfortable to me. To finance this project, I sold my quaint home that was almost paid off, liquidated my apartment complex that I was collecting rent on, and took on a huge loan to renovate my Temple. Moreover it required me to move from San Francisco, the city where I was born, to live by myself in an unfamiliar town and seedy neighborhood.

Never having been a business owner, I was virtually starting three enterprises at the same time and taking on all the responsibilities and risk that came with it. Every month required faith, tenacity and diligence to meet the payroll and payments. It's been a long journey with many ups and downs, yet I persevered through it all. Taking on this project had left me in debt

but it had made me richer in the process. I gained a richness of the soul that can never be taken away from me — the wisdom and experience I attained, the creativity I was able to express, and the level of strength and determination I acquired.

Suddenly, writing this book seemed much less daunting. If I can handle starting three businesses from scratch, I think I can handle writing a book about my experiences. I'm sure a publisher will provide me with a brilliant editor who will polish my words with eloquence, a gifted photographer will take gorgeous pictures, not to mention the food stylist, recipe tester, book designer, proofreader. With a slew of people helping me, how hard can it be? I guess ignorance is bliss. About two-thirds into writing my book, I started to research the feasibility of getting my book published. To my dismay, I found that even if by some miracle I was one of the lucky few to be accepted, it would take about two years before the book is actually published. Two years! I'm an entrepreneur at heart, and I knew I could personally do it in much less time. I ended up writing, editing and publishing the book myself. My restaurant manager Kin Ho and I took the snapshots to be included. With my head chef, Ricky Wong, we taste-tested the recipes and modified them for home use.

Gail Waldo, who rents an office in my Temple for her graphic arts business, beautifully designed the book layout. When I consider how many people it usually entails to publish a book, with the few that were involved here it demonstrates that you *can* accomplish anything if you set your mind and heart to it.

Thank you for taking a tour of my Temple through *Joy Meadow Cookbook: Recipes to Nourish the Body, Mind and Spirit*. I would be delighted to meet you in person and have you taste the savory delicacies prepared at Joy Meadow. While you are here, saunter through the Enchanted Garden and greet the flower fairies. Browse a book or two from Angel Light or partake in a class at the Temple of Light. I hope the book uplifts your soul and encourages you to live your highest dream.

Valencia Chan

May 2004

Recommended Reading

✍ Angels

Angelspeake: How to Talk to Your Angels, Barbara Mark and Trudy Griswold, Simon & Schuster, Inc. 1995

Archangels and Ascended Masters, Doreen Virtue, Hay House, Inc. 2003

Ask Your Angels, Alma Daniel, Timothy Wyllie, Andrew Ramer, Ballantine Books, 1992

Commune with the Angels, Jane M. Howard, A.R.E. Press, 1st Printing 1992, 10th Printing 2003

Healing with the Angels Oracle Cards, Doreen Virtue, Hay House, Inc. 1999

How to Work with Angels, Elizabeth Clare Prophet, Summit University Press, 1998

Inspired by Angels – Letters from the Archangel: Michael, Raphael, Gabriel and Uriel, Sinda Jordan, Blue Dolphin Publishing, 1995

One Hundred Ways to Attract Angels, Samara Anjelae, Red Wheel/Weiser, 2003

Working with Your Guides and Angels, Ruth White, Red Wheel/Weiser, 1997

✍ Animal Kingdom

Animal Magick, DJ Conway, Llewellyn Publishing, 1995

Animal Energies, Paul Horn, Dancing Otter Publishing, 1992

Animal Speak, Ted Andrews, Llewellyn Worldwide, 1993

Chinese Astrology: Ancient Secrets for Modern Life, Sabrina Liao, Warner Books, 2000

The Druid Animal Oracle, Phillip and Stephanie Carr-Gomm, Simon & Schuster, 1994

Medicine Cards, Jamie Sams and David Carson, St. Martin's Press, 1988

✍ Aromatherapy

Aromatherapy: A Complete Guide to the Healing Arts, Kathi Keville and Mindy Green, The Crossing Press, 1995

Complete Aromatherapy Handbook, Suzanne Fischer-Rizzi, Sterling Publishing, 1990

The Encyclopedia of Aromatherapy, Chrissie Wildwood, Healing Arts Press, 1996

✍ Astrology

Astrology and Relationship, David Pond, Llewellyn Worldwide, 2002

The Only Astrology Book You'll Ever Need, Joanna M. Woolfolk, Madison Books, 1982

Planets In Signs, Skye Alexander, Whitford Press, 1988

Pocket Guide to Astrology, Alan Oken, The Crossing Press, 1996

Transits: The Time of Your Life, Betty Lundsted, Red Wheel/Weiser 1980

✍ Crystals & Stones

Crystal Deva Cards, Cindy Watlington, Inner Quest Publishing, 1996

Color and Crystals: A Journey Through the Chakras, Joy Gardner Gordon, The Crossing Press, 1988

Cunningham's Encyclopedia of Crystal, Gem, and Metal Magic, Scott Cunningham, Llewellyn Worldwide, 1988

Illustrated Guide to Crystals, Judy Hall, Sterling Publishing Co., 2000

Love is In the Earth: A Kaleidoscope of Crystals, Melody, Earth Love Publishing House, 1995

✍ Feng Shui

Creating Sacred Space with Feng Shui, Karen Kingston, Broadway Books, 1997

Interior Design with Feng Shui, Sarah Rossbach, Penguin Group, 1987

Feng Shui Tips for a Better Life, David Daniel Kennedy, Storey Book, 1998

Sacred Space, Denise Linn, Ballantine Books, 1995.

Western Guide to Feng Shui, Terah Kathryn Collins, Hay House, Inc. 1996

✍ Flower Remedies

Bach Flower Remedies for Beginners, David F. Vennells, Llewellyn Worldwide, 2001

Flower Essence Repertory, Patricia Kaminski and Richard Katz, Flower Essence Society, 1987

Flower Remedies: Natural Healing with Flower Essences, Christine Wildwood, Element Books Limited, 1995

Little Book of Bach Flower Remedies, David Lord, Astrolog Publishing House, 1998

Pocket Guide to Bach Flower Essences, Rachelle Hasnas, The Crossing Press, 1997

✍ Nature Spirits & Fairies

Enchantment of the Faerie Realm, Ted Andrews, Llewellyn Publications, 1993

Deluxe Book of Flower Fairies, Cicely Mary Barker, Penguin Group, 2003

The Findhorn Garden, The Findhorn Community, Findhorn Press, 1975

Healing with the Fairies, Doreen Virtue, Hay House, Inc. 2001

Gnomes in the Garden, David and Carol Swing, Avalon Grove Press, 2003

Real World of Fairies, Dora Van Gelder, Theosophical Publishing House, 1st Printing 1977, reprinted 1999

To Live with the Fairy Folk, Marina T. Stern, Red Wheel/Weiser, 2002

World of Fairies, Gossamer Penwyche, Sterling Publishing Co. Inc., 2001

Recipe Index

Key: Description of dish 00,   *Photo of dish 00*,   **Recipe for dish 00**

General Index

To purchase a copy of ***Joy Meadow Cookbook: Recipes to Nourish the Body, Mind and Spirit***, check with your local bookstores.

Joy Meadow Cookbook: Recipes to Nourish the Body, Mind and Spirit is also available at Angel Light Books & Gifts and Joy Meadow Restaurant.

To order by phone, please call
(650) 780-9900
email angellightbooks@aol.com

To order by mail, please send $19.95 plus $3.95 for shipping and handling for one book, and $1.95 for each additional copy.

	QTY.		TOTAL
Books at $19.95 each	_____	× 19.95	_____
Shipping and handling for 1 copy	_____	× 3.95	_____
Shipping and handling for additional copies	_____	× 1.95	_____
	TOTAL AMOUNT ENCLOSED		_____

Please charge my: ☐ VISA   ☐ MASTER CARD   ☐ AMERICAN EXPRESS

NAME _____

ADDRESS _____

CITY / STATE / ZIP _____

PHONE_____   E-MAIL _____

CREDIT CARD NO. _____ EXP DATE _____

NAME AS IT APPEARS ON CREDIT CARD _____

SIGNATURE X_____

Make your check payable (and return) to:
Angel Light Books & Gifts
709 El Camino Real
Redwood City, CA 94063